HOW TO RENT

YOUR HOUSE, DUPLEX, TRIPLEX & OTHER MULTI-FAMILY PROPERTY FAST!

HOW TO RENT

YOUR HOUSE, DUPLEX, TRIPLEX & OTHER MULTI-FAMILY PROPERTY FAST!

The Concise Authoritative Owner's Manual for Rental Property with a Special Section on Airbnb Rentals

You will get 129 Simple Ways for Landlords to Fill Vacancies and a Whole Lot More

M. MITCH FREELAND

LAS VEGAS BOOK COMPANY

Las Vegas, Nevada

Copyright © 2018 by M. Mitch Freeland

Published by Las Vegas Book Company
Las Vegas, Nevada

SPECIAL SALES

Books published by Las Vegas Book Company are available at special quantity discounts worldwide to be used for sales training or for use in corporate promotional programs. Quantity discounts are available to corporations, educational institutions and charitable organizations. Personalized front or back covers endpapers can be produced in large numbers.

For information contact:
Email: MMitchFreeland@gmail.com   Website: www.MitchFreeland.com

1. Real Estate Investing 2. Business & Money 3. Property Management 4. Income Opportunities 5. Title: How to Rent Your House...

ISBN: 978-17241-1397-9

First Paperback Edition: September 29, 2018

ABOUT
M. MITCH FREELAND

M. Mitch Freeland has bought and sold, fixed and flipped hundreds of single-family and multi-family properties and has managed over 100 units as a landlord. He had been called "a modern-day polymath" due to the diversity of subjects that appeal to him and for the subjects he writes about. He is a person of faith, a business person, and a writer. He writes both fiction and nonfiction.

Mitch studied Anthropology at UCLA and started writing at forty-four. Since then, he has written sixty books and over two hundred articles and essays. Everything he writes about, he has experienced.

He has been an active investor in numerous young companies and start-ups dealing in all classes of investments for over twenty-five years. He was President and founder of an online bookstore, and current President and founder of a publishing company (Go-Getter Express). He was Managing Director of private Investment Banking companies, and a hands-on operator in his real estate investing and property management companies.

Regarding his nonfiction writing, his goal is to create intuitive, pertinent content that can be incorporated into your personal and work life to help you succeed faster and with less stress. Mitch's books are geared to getting you where you want to be faster, with a greater commitment for moving you safely and easily through all the unforeseen hurdles common and sometimes not so common with day to day business and life. Mitch makes the journey more enjoyable and fun. He gives you the short-cuts, the tips, the methods, and strategies that allow you speedy, secure and growing prosperity.

He has a new website and blog at www.MitchFreeland.com that focuses on strategies for motivation and personal development . He also writes about casino gaming, poker, real estate investing, online bookselling, Christianity and the Bible.

Selected Books by M. MITCH FREELAND

Real Estate Investing
The Millionaire Real Estate Flippers (New Edition)

High Engagement Landlording

How to Make Real Estate More Valuable

How to Rent you House, Duplex, Triplex & Other Multi-Family Property Fast!

The Real Estate Hustle

5 Day Flip: How to Get Offers Accepted Fast on Fixer-Uppers

Casino Gaming Books
Winning Craps: How to Play and Win Like a Pro. Learn How I Beat the Craps Out of the Casinos for 30 Years

Tested Gambling Systems That Can Make You $100,000+ a Year: Craps, Horses, Poker, Blackjack

How to Play Craps and Win: The 3 Irrefutable Winning Plays and How to Profit from Them

How to Win at Casino Craps

How to Play Baccarat

How to Count Cards at Blackjack

How to Play Blackjack for Beginners and Win! Learn Basic and Advanced Strategies for Optimum Winning Play

Poker Books
The Small Stakes Poker Hustle: How I Make $3,500+ A Month Part-Time Playing $1-$2 & $1-$3 No-Limit Hold'em & How You Can Too!

Poker Tells and Body Language: How to Substantially Improve Your Income by Studying Your Opponents Mannerisms and Eccentricities

Cash Poker: How to Make $250,000 Over the Next 5 Years Playing Small Stakes Poker

The Poker System: How to Play No-Limit Texas Hold'em: A Primer for Smart New Players Who Want to Start with A Winning Edge in the World's Greatest Poker Game

CONTENTS

Chapter 4: **Ancillary Income Part I 55**

Chapter 5: **Ancillary Income Part II**
Offering Upgrades 69

Introduction

The week before Christmas last year, I was cleaning out several shelves of books and came across a number of books on real estate investing and landlording. Most of the books I had purchased about fifteen years ago when my brother and I decided to get involved heavily in real estate investing. Over the course of eight years we purchased, renovated and flipped dozens of properties. And there were other properties which we fixed and rented—some for many years to steady paying tenants.

As I went through the books that I had once studied I realized not one of them dealt exclusively with getting vacant property rented—and getting them renting quickly to solid tenants. Of course, landlords do the natural things such as placing a "For Rent" sign in the yard and perhaps running a couple of ads in the local paper or online have worked in the past. Does this still work? Sure it does, but now with the internet there are dozens of outlets for getting the word out on your property. What you need is mass distribution of information to attract the best possible tenants. As we know, there are millions of lousy tenants out there and you certainly do not want them in your rentals. You want long-term, steady-as-she-goes, tenants who pay on time and advise you early of any problems. Renting properties is serious business—not to be taken lightly. I reflected back on the renters I had; the good ones, the bad ones and the really bad ones, and decided to do something about it. Thus, the creation of this book was hatched.

Marketing your rentals for quality tenants is not a science, it is not an art, there is no special formula, and I am no genius—far from it. It is, however, a doable exercise, one which is much easier when you work at it with what I like to call *creative distribution of information*. What is creative distribution of information? It's no more than getting the word out and getting it out fast that you have great rental property available for the right price.

Every day that your property does not have a tenant in it paying rent is a day you are losing money. The faster you get the word out in your community about your great available vacancies, the sooner you will be making, and not losing, money. Attracting the right, quality tenant is paramount. How nice it is when you have a tenant who stays in your rental for ten years, paying on time every month, and never complains about a rent hike—at least not to you.

The lack of adequate cash flow is the number one reason real estate investors get in trouble. And by having a solid tenant will alleviate many of the problems that can arise over the years.

Fishing for Tenants

Not long ago I met an old man who was shore fishing. He had laid out on the sand five Pompano, each weighing about five to fifteen pounds. They were nice looking fish and as I learned from the old man, he had been coming to the same spot for the past three days to fish. You see, every day for the past week at around 3 o'clock a school of Pompano came in close to shore to feed. You could see the bait fish in enormous schools thrashing and jumping out of the water. The water was boiling, as a seasoned fisherman would say—a frenzy of Pompano and millions of bait fish. The Pompano were gorging.

The Pompano were about thirty feet out from where the surf broke. All one had to do is cast a lure or a hook full of bait in this area and the chance of getting a hookup was practically guaranteed. Go where the fish are. If you have eyes and you keep them open, and you have at least the common sense of a fish, you will catch fish—go were the fish are. Concentration in this area will produce strong results.

12

Another way of fishing productively is to drop your line in several different areas and trying each over a vast expansion of water front. Now, when you get a bite you begin to focus in on that specific place betting on a large school to be in a concentrated area.

The smartest of the fishermen uses a net and gets everything in the area. Once the nets are pulled in, the small and undesirable fish are tossed back and the best, the biggest are kept.

A fisherman fishes for fish and a landlord fishes for tenants. You go where you can to capture the highest number of prospective tenants in the shortest period of time. In many areas you can be selective of the tenant you choose. In other areas, blighted or transitional sections of town may not allow you the comforts of solid tenants—here you will have to be patient and study every applicant closely.

When you are after fish or tenants, the process is pretty much the same. The small ones get thrown back and the big fish, the best are kept. To get the best tenants, like fish, you cast your nets wide.
Happy fishing!

M. Mitch Freeland
Los Angeles, CA

Chapter 1

A Few Rules Starting Out

"The price of success is hard work, dedication to the job at hand, and the determination that whether we win or lose, we have applied the best of ourselves to the task at hand."
—Vince Lombardi

When my brother John and I formed a real estate investment club several years ago, we found that the biggest deterrent of people getting involved and investing in rental property was the fear they had of not being able to rent their property and to attain good paying tenants. Many people wanted to own rental property. High cash flow and the strong real estate market gave many the motivation to try something; however, dealing the thought of vacancies and tenants, and the problems they might create, kept most out of the game. This is understandable. Many aspiring landlords do not know how to go about getting tenants to fill vacancies, and many simply do not want to deal with tenants—or the possibility of tenant confrontations. Thinking about the perpetual vacancy—the unit(s) that never get filled, and having, unfortunately that alligator chewing down the cash flow can certainly be a negative concept of an ill-conceived plan.

Many beginning investors are also very concerned with not attracting and renting to the proverbial problem tenant. The question remains, what to do with a vacant rental and what if I can't get it rented? "I would rather hire a rental agency to take care of all that," was a common response to many investment club members.

My brother and I were always hands-on, so getting an agency to manage our 100 plus units was never even brought up as a serious concern.

With a few solid moves you could have your rentals (vacancies) filled quickly. All you have to do is move fast and be creative—and be flexible.

The trick to all sales and getting vacant units leased is to make it easy for your prospective customer (tenant) to say yes. Offer the customer what they need and then give them what they want. You have to do the selling—and make the sale. Be open, be creative and ask questions, narrowing down the prospects concerns—then go for the close. Simply don't show the property. Ask questions and make the close. Get the prospect involved with your property the moment she steps foot in the parking area. Paint an indelible picture for the prospect—and make it easy for her to say yes. Tell the features, explain all the benefits—ask the questions—make the close—sign the lease.

When I first started with landlording, one of my first properties was a vacant building of 16 units. Naturally, it was a fixer upper and all 16 units needed immediate updating: carpets, tile, paint, replacement of door locks and the usual fix-up stuff. The exterior of the property also needed the necessary esthetics to show well to prospective tenants—mostly paint and clean-up, landscaping and a new sign.

As each unit was repaired it was leased. The apartment was on a busy street, a major thoroughfare, and this helped greatly because of the high visibility. *For Lease* signs were posted in front of the property and prospective tenants called and appointments for showing the units were made. The units were fully leased in thirty days after completion of fix up. The tenant base was mixed will mostly lower income, Hispanic and black tenants. There was room for a laundry room with one washer and dryer, bringing in about $240 a month. We also placed a Pepsi machine near the laundry room which brought in $60 a month.

The 16 unit building was in a lower income neighborhood, as noted, and now completely fixed up, it was the best on the block and this is why tenants floated in quickly.

As the years passed, we purchased, rehabbed and rented dozens of properties: single family homes, duplexes, triplexes, many multi-family properties. We set the rents and leased the properties to families and singles alike. The number one source to attract tenants has always been the yard sign, *For Rent*.

All signs used on multi-family properties were meant to be hung permanently. We used an eight foot long post with a two sided swinging sign with the company name and a large phone number—just like the types of signs real estate agents use when selling a house. These signs were left up permanently on all of our multi-family properties even when we were fully leased up.

1.1

When you get a call from a prospective tenant and the inquiry is for a property that is leased up, you can direct the prospect to your other vacancies at different locations. If everything you have is leased, you can now direct the prospect to other landlords and receive a commission (one full month's rent) as payment for leasing their property. Here you will have to secure an agreement as finder for the landlord prior to showing it to prospects, or if you are a licensed real estate agent or broker, you have a way of making more income.

1.2

This sign is for permanent use. It is posted on the property permanently. We state in the sign that there are 1, 2, 3 & 4 bedrooms. The sign is designed to get calls from anybody looking for 1 to 4 bedrooms. Whether we have any of these available or not, we will get the call, get the names, and qualify the prospective renters. If we do not have vacancies, we will turn the prospect to other properties that are available. Not only will we get a commission from the other property owner, when leased, but we will also keep a copy of the application. When the lease is up, contact the tenant and ask if they are happy where they are and then explain the benefits of your property if you have a vacancy.

By keeping a file of your non tenants, you know when leases are expiring, income levels, credit worthiness, and all the other necessary information that distinguishes a prospective, solid tenant. You should keep a tenant email list

18

and every time a unit becomes available you can email the new listing. It is important that you also have your own website with a list of properties and units available. These non-tenants can go on your Christmas card and birthday card list and any other holiday card list. By staying in contact, you now have the opportunity to service their future rental needs. This also allows you the opportunity to ask for referrals of people, friends, or relatives who might be moving soon.

A Few Rules I Learned From the Beginning:

1. Get the *For Rent* or *For Lease* sign out early—right when you acquire the property—even before you start the rehab and cleanup work. Many times you will have your house or apartment rented prior to the rehab being completed. You start receiving income immediately.

2. If the property is multi-family, post the *For Rent* sign out front of the building permanent.

3. Use multiple signs with large properties and properties that sit on a corner. Place signs that can be seen from all street directions.

4. Visit your local Housing Authority (Section 8) office prior to closing on any new property. Fill out the forms and get ready.

5. Have rental applications ready. Have the leases ready.

6. Charge a rental application fee of $25. If the market can justify a greater fee, use your judgment. A $40 application fee could also be suitable. Most people in lower income areas will pay cash. However, if cash is not available, a convenient tool to have is the *Square* (www.Square.com). The *Square* allows you to take credit/debit cards wherever you are. You swipe the card into the insert that goes on your mobile phone (you can also use a tablet). It is super easy to use—it's fast, and I highly recommend it. And it is free. The current charge is 2.75 percent per swipe and covers MasterCard, Visa, Discover and American Express. Naturally, cash is the best way to

go—but if cash is not available use this convenient devise to lock the prospect down on the application so you can begin the process of checking references. Don't forget to charge the prospect 2.75 percent more for the transaction. Paypal and Amazon have a similar service.

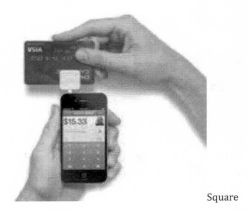

Square

7. Have rental agreements ready with one or two year lease minimum.

8. Always collect full first, last and security deposit at signing of lease. No exceptions.

9. Do not hand over keys until all cash is received or checks have cleared your bank.

10. Always try to get more than one person to sign the lease. Have **all adults** that will be living on your property sign the lease.

11. Get Steel custom signs made.

1.3

1.4

If you are in the acquisition mode, get steel signs posted on your properties quickly. Remove all signs when single-family houses are leased, but keep your signs up permanently with your multi-family properties. Why should you keep your signs posted on multi-family properties when you are leased-up? There are several reasons for this:

1) When prospective renters call, you share with them other rentals you have available that are in the general area.

2) You collect a data base of people who you can call for future vacancies. You call as soon as a vacancy occurs.

3) You show them units from other landlords in the area and take a finders commission or one full month's rent when leased. Here you will need an agreement with a number of landlords in your area.

The sign above (1.4) is designed so a phone number or email address could be attached to the top or bottom. Photo 1.3 illustrates this with a smaller steel sign attached on top. Photo 1.1 shows the attached sign to the bottom of the *For Rent* sign.

Keep Lease In-Hand and Clipboard Close

As soon as you get out of your car and step foot on your property you should have your rental application ready for the prospective tenant, a copy of the standard lease you use and other flyers and documents explaining the property for rent and the rules regarding parking, laundry, noise, etc. The application should be attached to a clipboard with a pen for your prospective tenant to fill-out. When you have a moment, I suggest that you acquire the book ***The Millionaire Real Estate Landlords.*** This book covers, in depth, hands-on property management with many step-by-step procedures for successful landlords. I wrote the book with my brother John, to help landlords capture not only more cash flow that seems to be left on the table, but also to help landlords become more effective and to help with their operations to become more fluid with less stress and headaches. As with all of my books, you can get a copy from Amazon (eBook or paperback) or from my website **www.MitchFreeland.com**

When you have your mobile phone or a computer with you, you can do a quick search of the tenant and make a few phone calls; references, employer and former landlords. You do not want to waste any time. Get everything done right there at the property. Your car can be your mobile office. Have the prospective tenant investigate the unit while you do your research.

- Employer and income check
- Credit check
- Former landlords
- References
- Others who will cosign on lease (students or young people may not have established credit history and other references; therefore, get parent or others to be added to the application and cosign on the lease. The more people to sign the lease, the better.

A Few Important Questions to Ask a Prospect

- How many people will be moving in? Children? Children will bring in more income due to ancillary income (Chapter 5)
- When would you like to move in?
- Have you any pets? (Naturally, you charge pet rent which is $15 to $25 per month more depending on size of pet)
- Do you want a 12 or 24 month lease?
- What is your budget?

Why You Can't Get it Rented

There can be countless reasons that your property isn't getting rented. In this section I have listed most of those reasons. Study them and assess the problems with your property. Inspect your property and inspect yourself. Write down all the things you have to do now to get your property and your business in top shape for quality long-term tenants.

- Rent price is too high (fixable)

- Property is not maintained (fixable)
- Repairs need to be made inside unit (fixable)
- Unit needs paint and updating (fixable)
- Your rental is in the ghetto (you can't do much here)
- Unit is filthy (fixable—clean it!)
- No appliances included (fixable)
- No air-conditioning (fixable)
- No parking (usually not fixable)
- You do not have a good rental sign. Rental sign is thrashed and phone number cannot be read. (fixable)
- Scummy current tenant base (fixable)
- No laundry facility (most times fixable)
- Bad location—far from everything (not fixable)
- Too noisy (depends on type of noise—fixable)
- Overbearing landlord—too many stupid rules (fixable)
- Landlord or on-sight property manager is creepy (fixable)
- Unsafe building or area / No security (fixable)
- Termites, roaches or other infestations (fixable)
- Leaky faucets or toilet (fixable)
- Leaky roof (fixable)

Many of the problems you face for having vacant units are fixable. Step back and take a good solid look at your property. Take notes of the exterior building, the grounds, and jot down ideas as to making the property from the outside more appealing. Sometimes it may only need minor clean up or touch up paint work. When you have finished with the outside begin with the inside. In most situations, you could have your property in tip-top shape in a day or two. Spend a little time and make the property attractive.

There are three kinds of landlords: (1) the landlord who is completely hands-off and hires a property management company to handle everything—too much money is being left on the table here and your costs shoot way up; (2) the landlord who is nearly hands off and does not keep his property maintained and thus charges low rent and attracts bottom of the barrel tenants; and (3) the landlord who is proactive, hands-on, with well

24

maintained properties and gets top rent with solid tenants who stay for years. I strongly urge you to be the latter. Proactive landlords bring in more cash, have tenants who are reliable and maintain their properties to ensure strong resale value with steady forced appreciation.

Chapter 2

Advertisements

"What really decides consumers to buy or not to buy is the content of your advertising, not its form."
—David Ogilvy

A dvertising online at selective sites and in local newspapers is sometimes all it takes to get a slew of interested renters.

Craigslist.org

One of the first places to go for advertising your vacancy is Craigslist.org. Here you can post a free announcement about your rental property. Not only can you list in your city but you can list in other areas as well. It is good practice to list your vacancies in nearby areas of up to twenty miles away. You can also list in larger cities or metropolitan areas, College and University towns and so on.

City Newspaper Classifieds

This includes your local city's online edition as well. Some small town papers may not be worth the price of advertising. Most city newspaper classifieds are worth the while with their online capability.

Some great bargains in real estate can still be had with classified ads when you are looking for an investment. Many older landlords have not succumbed to the internet and how to advertise with it.

Free Papers, Thrifty Penny, Nifty Nickel

Every community has free papers who survive with the constant baiting of advertisers. Typically, in front of your supermarket, Wal-Mart store, or the public library, you will find a number of local free papers. The cost for advertizing is low and sometimes free depending on the aims of the paper.

Ethnic Newspapers

America is indeed a melting pot of ethnicity, cultures and religions. Many communities in the U.S. have pockets of Chinese, Vietnamese, Jews, and Hispanics making up communities as China Town, Little Saigon, and others. When you have property in or adjacent to a very specific cultural area it can be a worthwhile mission to market in their local papers.

Don't worry about not knowing the language or how to read or write in Spanish or Vietnamese, the people in the advertizing department will translate your advertisement.

Hispanic Papers

Hispanic papers seem to be everywhere; and some are paid papers. Many parts of the country are dominated by Hispanics where English is a second language. If your rentals are in lower income areas, or predominantly rental areas, it is most likely you have a potential draw of Hispanic tenants. Places like Huntington Park, in Los Angele County are on of many municipalities that carry a residential population of over 90% Hispanic. Man these communities can be great rental opportunities.

Cuban Papers

If you have rental property in South Florida you will come across a number of papers designed for the Cuban population. Many of the papers are free.

Jewish Papers

Where there is a large Jewish population you will get free Jewish papers. Certain areas of Southern California and Los Angeles, Boca Raton, Florida, and New York city to name a few have a number of papers.

Chinese & Vietnamese Papers

Here again, when your rentals are in or near Chinese or Vietnamese areas you will find free newspapers and magazines for advertising.

We've examined some of the ways you can advertise in local newspapers and magazines. Going forward we will examine a list of 95 other ways and ideas. We won't need to go into much detail here since many of the ideas presented are straight forward and involve posting flyers or cards advertizing your property for rent. Flyers are typically 8.5" x 11" sheets of copy paper (yellow pages with black print stands out the best—think of Western Union colors).

Posted cards can be index cards, 3" x 5" or 4" x 6".

The one thing you always want to keep mindful of, and probably the most important thing, is keeping cost down. No need to pay for advertising when you do not have to. There are lots of free papers, websites and ways to advertise without investing a dime.

Real Estate Rental Agencies

Probably the most expensive way to get a tenant is from a real estate rental agency. Most agents expect one full month's rent as commission on a year lease. If the agent secures a tenant for your rental house and your rental house is rented for $2,000 per month, the agent will receive $2,000 as commission. This is expensive, and for most landlords an unnecessary waste of a lot of money. However, if you are not the rent collector type, you can also contract a property management company to collect your rents.

The List

I had compiled a list of sixty-eight resources that can be used to get tenants. As you read the list of rental ideas, jot down the places that are near your property first, and make those your first priority. Remember, all it takes one good tenant who will stay for years.

I have had tenants who have stayed for over eight and more years. After I had bought and sold the property years later, they remained. I have known landlords who have had great tenants who have remained for fifteen years and many with tenants who have remained for over twenty years—faithfully paying rent month after month with occasional increases to rent for adjustments to account for inflation and gentrification, which in boom times creates strong property appreciation.

I won't go into detail of all the items in this list, since I feel they are self explanatory and you will, for the most part, need to create a flyer or card to post your rental vacancy.

I have included a few examples of flyers and signs, bulletin board postings, business cards you ought to have, and other types of brochures and handouts to draw out prospective tenants.

Printed Papers and Newsletters

1. Recycler/Recyler.com
2. Real Estate Monthlies
3. Local area Free papers—every community has one or more free papers.
4. College Newspapers
5. Advertise in sports programs for local events (little leagues, high school, etc.)
6. Advertise in Housing Authority (Section 8)
7. Advertise in corporate newsletters and mailer

Bulletin boards

8. Super Market Bulletin boards
9. Small neighborhood grocers
10. Neighborhood doughnut shops
11. Bowling alleys
12. College Bulletin Boards
13. Senior Centers
14. Libraries
15. Parks and Recreation
16. Laundromat Bulletin Boards
17. Your properties bulletin boards
18. Large company bulletin boards (human resource department)
19. Post flyers at the local Housing Authority/get on the Housing Authority list by offering Section 8 Housing.
20. Post flyers at other state, county and city housing departments
21. Post flyers with non-profit private organizations that pay for rent for down and outers
22. Post at churches and other houses of worship
23. Post with local merchants
24. Post with your Chamber of Commerce. Also with flyers and emails.
25. Organizations and clubs you are a member
26. Boys and Girls club
27. YMCA

Postings and Handouts

28. Posting flyer in your laundry room
29. Handing out flyers to current tenants
30. Handing out flyers at local Laundromats
31. Posting flyers at dry-cleaning stores
32. Handing out flyers in your neighborhood
33. Handing out flyers at your real estate investment club meetings
34. Posting flyers at restaurants
35. Handout flyers to neighbors
36. Truck rental and moving companies
37. Furniture rental stores

Signage

38. Have a For Rent sign posted on property
39. Post signs at busy intersections
40. Post signs on all of your properties
41. Post lawn signs in English and Spanish
42. Post a sign on your car
43. Car Magnets
44. Put a large banner on the property
45. Billboards

Incentivizing Current Tenants

46. Get testimonials from current tenants and ask for referrals
47. Pay finders fees of 5% or 10% of first month's rent
48. Discounts on rent and the holiday season
49. Pay commissions to non tenants who make referrals (get the word out)

Police and Firefighters

50. Visit police and fire stations and handout flyers and post on bulletin boards

Create Incentives for Renters

51. Offer a gift (toaster, $20 gift card to a supermarket, etc.)
52. Free rent (month 13 free with a 12 month lease)
53. Discounted Rent (10% off for December rent)
54. Coupons
55. Pizza at move-in
56. Referral for double leases
57. Longer term lease incentives (month 25 free with a 2 year lease)

Promotional Items

58. Business cards that say "I have a place for You"
59. Pins or buttons "I have a place for you."

60. Wear a t-shirt or collared polo or oxford with embroidery "I rent from a great landlord—Do you want his number?"
61. Give a t-shirt to renters when they move in. "I rent from a great landlord" call 800-555-5555.

Mailing Campaigns
62. Send post cards or letters to renters throughout the city
63. Send letters / call other landlords for referrals
64. Send letters to teachers, professionals, police and fire-fighters

Real Estate Agents and Others
65. Contact real estate agents (remember you will be paying a commission to a licensed agent)
66. Rental agencies (commission will have to be paid-usually one full month of rent)
67. Insurance agents
68. Law offices

Summing Up
With a little creative imagination and with your eyes fully opened, you can now see countless ways to get the word out about your available rental. The sixty-eight items listed will help spark your imagination to pursue other formerly unrecognized sources in your community for marketing.

There is no doubt that if you implement just five of the sources noted, you will have your choice of tenants. Choose the sources of marketing that best suits your location and begin. In less than one day you could have your vacancy filled.

Chapter 3

Salesmanship and Online Resources

I've found that luck is quite predictable. If you want more luck, take more chances. Be more active. Show up more often.
—Brian Tracy

It doesn't matter what we do—we are selling. We are selling something to someone everyday of our lives—believe it or not.

What Works Best

According to the National Association of Realtors, 40 percent of buyers and renters come from the Multiple Listing Service; 20 percent from signs; 18 percent responded to an advertisement, but purchased or rented a different property; 8 percent responded to an open house, but purchased a different home; 7 percent went through a relocation service, 3 percent bought an advertised property; 3 percent bought from a combination of mediums; and only 1 percent bought a house from an open house they attended.

The evidence is clear you should first list your property on the MLS, Loopnet.com, and Airbnb.com. And to move your merchandise, you should incorporate a plan of marketing by using all the resources available to you. If you hire a realtor, get in writing what he/she will do to market your property, whether renting or selling. If you decide to rent on your own, you should use as many of the resources listed in this book.

This section is filled with ideas on renting your property and marketing your property effectively. Review your options and do as much as you can. Much of your marketing campaign will not be difficult to execute, but it is time consuming, so you will need to make the time and put your plan down in writing.

Other Internet Sites

There are many websites you could list your property on for more exposure. Many websites have fees for listing your rental properties. Other sites such as Craigslist.org are free in many areas.

Check out the following websites for listing your rentals:

69. HotPads.com (Free)
70. Craigslist.org (Free in many places)
71. Trulia.com (Free)
72. Oodle.com (Free)
73. Vast.com (Free)
74. RentDigs.com (Free)
75. ForRent.com
76. RentJungle.com
77. Streeteasy.com (not in all areas)
78. Alexa.com
79. Rent.com
80. Rentals.com
81. Realtor.com
82. Homesforrent.com
83. Everyrent.com
84. RentalHouses.com
85. Appfolio.com
86. Homeaway.com (vacation rentals)
87. Airbnb.com (vacation rentals)
88. Scenicrentals.com petvr.com (vacation rentals)

89. rentalspot.com (vacation rentals)
90. findyourvacationhome.com (vacation rentals)
91. dwellable.com (vacation rentals)
92. adventurepads.com (vacation rentals)
93. fhbo.com (vacation rentals)
94. escapelets.com (vacation rentals)
95. trekkvacations.com (vacation rentals)
96. qualityvacationrental.com (vacation rentals)
97. Snowbirdseeker.com (vacation rentals)
98. Local.com
99. RealRenters.com
100. Apartments.com
101. Loopnet.com
102. Rentlinx.com
103. RealEstate.com
104. Yahoo Real Estate
105. eBay.com
106. AltaVista.com
107. Livingchoices.com
108. RealEstatebook.com
109. Homeagain.com
110. Houselocator.com
111. Homepages.com
112. Realestatejournal.com
113. Realtytrac.com
114. Condo.com
115. Areaguides.net
116. Zillow.com (Free)
117. Twitter.com (Free)
118. Instagram.com (Free)
119. Yelp.com
120. Facebook.com (Free)

With fifty-one websites to list your vacancies you have plenty to choose from. Naturally, you will list on the "free" sites first. If you have rentals in and around New York City you can also try this site:

121. Nakedapartments.com

For vacation and short-term rentals by owner try these sites:

122. VRBO.com (Vacation Rentals by Owner)
123. Airbnb.com
124. HomeAway.com (Vacation Rentals)
125. Wimdu.com
126. Roomaramma.com (Vacation Rentals)
127. HotelTonight.com
128. Couchsurfing.com
129. 9Flats.com

The vacation and short-term rental market, with the advent of Airbnb, HomeAway.com and VRBO.com has established a new and exploding income generation system for landlords willing to take the leap. A well positioned rental and a highly engaged landlord can increase current income by 100% to 300%. Offering a unique experience for short-term tenants is on the rise. When you incorporate a reasonable price with a first class experience you will receive the results you expect.

I am in the process of completing *The Airbnb Hustle: How Ordinary People and Enterprising Landlords are Cashing-in and How you can Too!* The book release date is Spring 2019. I suggest that if you are interested in learning more about increasing your income substantially on short-term rentals get a copy. Here is a quick rundown what you will get:

In *The Airdbnb Hustle*, you will discover:

- How to cash in on your rental propety with spectacular short-term income.
- How to get stellar, 5 STAR reviews
- Everything you need to get started
- How to double and triple your current income
- How to replicate a growing business model
- How to make money by not owning any property
- How to present an award winning listing

- How to price rooms for holidays and big events
- How to explode your income with ancilary services and products
- How to promote your rentals like a professional
- How to stage each room for that spa feeling
- How to prepare welcome packages with forms, brochuures and local discounts that your tenants will love
- How to deliver over-the-top service that guaranttees positive reviews, repeat guests and referrals
- How to resolve problems stress free
- How to manage property when you are not in town

Short-term rentals might be the fit your looking for.

As noted earlier, studies have shown that over 80% of renters will search the internet first before contacting a rental agent to help in their rental search. Therefore, it is extremely important to have your listing on the MLS, Zillow.com and Craigslist.com.

Descriptive Words Renters Want to Hear

I've borrowed much of the information here from my book *The Millionaire Real Estate Landlords*. Whether you are marketing to buyers or renters most people want to hear many of the same things. Make it a habit to incorporate the following words or phrases into your ad copy and conversation with prospective renters. Professional selling is all about using the correct words to get your message across to renters. Remember, one good word could trigger a potential renter to becoming a long lease customer.

- Quiet Neighborhood
- Highly rated School District
- Discover Tranquility
- Exclusive Neighborhood
- Children Friendly Neighborhood

- Family Comforts
- Park Like or Country Like yard
- Lush setting
- Easy Maintenance or low maintenance.
- Private Setting
- Close to shopping and restaurants
- Ocean views, lake views, park views, greenbelt views, or mountain views, open views.
- Spacious living areas
- Large rooms
- Naturally sun-filled rooms
- Home warranty
- Chefs kitchen with gourmet amenities
- Bathroom fit for royalty
- Energy saving appliances
- Pride of the block
- Like a model
- Enjoy Extra income
- Ample room for RV or boat
- Location, location…
- Comfort and intimacy
- Live in style
- Stately and impressive grounds
- Breathtaking views
- Prestigious neighborhood
- Tree-lined street
- Lovingly remodeled
- Lots of built-in
- Cozy and charming hideaway
- Hilltop views
- Vibrant neighborhood
- Private and secluded
- Up-and-coming neighborhood
- Ideally located
- Priced to rent fast
- Storybook cottage

- Elegantly appointed
- Country living at its best
- Country charm
- Built with quality from a bygone era
- New Appliances (Stainless Steel Appliances)
- Easy walking to shopping and Bus stop

Prepping Your Property to Rent

This is a simple, yet effective approach:

- Keep it clean. This is the number one prerequisite prior to showing your property to prospective tenants.

- Get to the property half hour before your scheduled showing and clean up paper, clean off counters, check lights, open blinds and remove any evidence of bugs

- If it is winter and it is cold and there is a fireplace, build a crackling fire

- If it is the dead of summer and 100 degrees, turn the air conditioner(s) on

- Flush toilets—ensure that they are spotless

- Keep the lid down on toilets if they are temporarily stained with hard water deposits or other stains

- Dust off all areas, smudges on doors and cabinets, appliances and cook-tops

- Keep windows (inside and outside) and shades clean

Showing the Property Correctly

When an interested party calls about seeing the house or apartment, set an appointment, preferably the same day while the sun is still shining. Set a time to meet and get to the property at least thirty minutes early to prepare the property for lease. When you are prepared, the renting will be easy. Here are a few things to do—some we've mentioned before:

1. *Turn all the lights on in every room*. The house has to be bright. And if there are ceiling fans with lights, turn the fans on low; show that the fans work. And make sure the fans run quietly.

2. *When it is warm, turn the air conditioning on*. The house should be comfortable inside. Turn the A/C on and set it at 72 degrees. If it is cold outside and the house is bone chilling inside, set the heating up to 75 degrees. If there is a fireplace, definitely start it. A roaring fire becomes quit cozy to look at on a very cold day.

3. *Make sure the floor in clean*. Clean any smudges or dirt off the floor. A wet cloth or sponge with a spray bottle of cleaner or Windex will do the job. You should also wipe off any fingerprints or smudges left on doors, cabinets and appliances. Don't forget to broom off the front and back porches and steps of leaves and dirt.

4. *Wipe down countertops and dirty windows*. Wipe down all counter tops in the kitchen and bath and all other places were dust and dirt accumulate. Use Windex or Glass-Plus on mirrors and windows, should they need cleaning. Mirrors should be crystal clean.

5. *Make sure toilets and sinks are clean*. Check each toilet in the house and if dirty clean it. Use bleach in a spray bottle with half water and a toilet brush for a quick clean, then flush. Keep the toilet seat down. Water stains in sinks and tubs should be cleaned off and the entire area dry.

6. *Prepare blinds or curtains to hang correctly*. Many times blinds and curtains are not positioned correctly to enhance the window. Make sure the blinds are even and not lopsided. The actual blind panels should be pointing

out and slightly downward at a 45 degree angle. This prevents the sun from entering into the room strongly. It also allows you to see out and prevents others from outside to see in. And, it lets in the right amount of sunlight to warm the room. You should use tiebacks for opening curtains or get a decorative ribbon and tie a bow in the center of it.

7. *Place scented candles in the bath and kitchen.* You could buy scented candles that are about 3 inches high; some will come in a round grass container. You can purchase most of your candles at dollar stores for one dollar, of course. Place one candle in each bathroom and light it before the buyers arrive; do the same with the kitchen. Some good scents that we've received positive comments on are vanilla, apple pie, and pumpkin pie. During the winter months those scents are warm and inviting. In summer, you could try lavender, watermelon, or peach scented candles. Rose scented candles have proven high on the complement list as well.

8. *Spray the house with a pleasant scent.* If you don't have candles, you can get an air freshener and spray each room. We do not recommend the type that plugs into the outlet and releases its scent; they are expensive and give off a very chemically enhanced odor. Lavender or rose is a good choice, it you are going to use an air freshener spray

Because it is important for you to know how to market your rental correctly, I've enclosed the following sections from the book ***The Millionaire Real Estate Flippers*** . The sections included are: "Make it Easy," "Qualifying the Buyer," which I've changed here to "Qualifying the Renter." The concepts are the same. Other subjects which we will cover are "Salesmanship," "More About Selling," "Property Facts Sheet," and "Twelve Most Common Renter Objections."

Becoming proactive in the selling of your properties will lead you to more deals and you will come in contact with more buyers and sellers in your target area--buyers that you might benefit from in the future, and sellers whose motives may let you acquire great property at good prices.

Make it Easy to Rent

To be at the top of your game, you have to be proactive, and you have to make it as easy as possible for the customer to say 'Yes, we'll take it.'

To help with the renting process, you must have a lease with you at all times and shows the prospective renters that this is your standard lease. When you first meet the renter, hand the application and lease to him or her—and have the renter carry the lease and the application. This will cut through all doubt in the renter's mind that your meeting today will end up with the signing of an agreement to lease property. You should ask lots of questions to narrow down the prospects concerns. Moreover, you should always have the prospect participate in the showing. What do I mean by this? It's simple. Have the prospect turn a light or ceiling fan on, then off, open a closet door or turn or adjust the blinds. Have the prospect touch and glide their hand over the granite countertops. Have the prospect open cabinets and closets. Get the prospect active and then start asking questions. The one who asks the questions, is the one who is in control.

Another way to get a renter involved is to give her a pad of paper on a clipboard and ask the her to write down all the things she does not like about the house or apartment. This will enable you to answer objections. For example, if a prospect wrote down, "Small Kitchen," your response could be: "A small kitchen is easier to clean and saves a lot of time, especially if you have a large family and your days are busy ones. How large of a family do you have?" Or, you could ask, "Oh, do you do a lot of cooking? If you do, a smaller kitchen makes cleanup a lot easier." After the prospect has spent some time walking through the unit and has not written anything down, you could then ask: "It looks like you like everything. Would you like to go ahead and fill out the application?" The prospects blank sheet of paper allows you an opportunity to go for a close.

You can also have the prospect draw a line down the center of the paper and at the top write "Dislike" on the left side of the paper and "Like" on the right side. Ask the prospect to write down everything she does not like about the property on the "Dislike" side and everything she likes on the "Like" side. The 'Likes" will typically outnumber the "Dislikes" three to one or better.

Now, review each "Dislike" with the prospect. These are the objections. Once you know all the objections, you overcome them one by one. The most common objections and how to overcome them are listed further along in this chapter.

Qualifying the Renter

It is very important to qualify the renter. You do not want to waste your time with people who are "just looking." You are interested in a motivated renter—someone who is ready to sign a lease now. You should ask renters candidly: "If you like what you see, are you ready to move in today?" The answer will cut through a lot of speculation on your part, and at the same time, clarify the renters intention. If the renters (Mr. and Mrs. Gotcashnow) say "yes," you've now locked them in—they are serious. If the renters say "no," you should then ask, "Why are you here today?" Again, you are probing for their true interest in the property. This should, preferably, be done over the phone before you meet at the property. Renters should always be qualified before you meet with them at the property. Ask what their budget is for rent.

As a matter of routine, you should ask as many questions as you can to expose the renters seriousness in and the level of their motivation. By asking questions, you are getting them involved. A professional salesperson knows by asking qualifying questions he or she controls the situation and the pace of the sale.

Here are questions to ask:

o   What is your price range?
o   What can you afford monthly?
o   How is your credit and what is is your credit score?
o   Do you have references?
o   Why are you looking for a new place?
o   How long have you been looking for a home/apartment?
o   Do you have a car?
o   How many kids do you have? How old are they?
o   Are you new to the area?

o   Are you ready to move-in immediately? Or, how soon can   you move?

Asking and Answering Questions

When you are showing the house/apartment, watch the prospects closely. Try to keep the prospects together (the children too) as you want to hear what they say and see the expressions they give to each other. Always state: "I am here to answer all of your questions." That is the only statement you should make. All other statements should be in the form of a question. You need to ask questions to get the answers, to sell. Watch how the buyers look at the kitchen and bathrooms and listen to what they say to each other. Then ask, "Do you like the bathroom?" By asking questions, you are getting the prospects involved. Remember, the prospects must be active in the selling process and they must be involved in demonstrating (showing) the property to themselves. You are not selling them anything--the buyers have to sell themselves first on the property.

Never ask "What do you think?" Instead, you should ask: "How do you feel about the color?" The buying process for most of us is emotional. Ask how the prospect feels, not what he or she thinks. Ask: "Doesn't this kitchen make you feel like cooking?" Or try: "That floor is original golden oak; it really makes the home feel warm, doesn't it? Do you like it?"

All great salesmen and women are sincere and enthusiastic about their product. And since you are the property owner you definitely know a great deal about the it. The more you know about your product, the more confident you are, and the more confident you are, the more enthusiastic you become. So, know your product and be enthusiastic about it. By the way, being enthusiastic does not always mean you are vocally and physically excited. But it does mean you are confident, proud and sincere about your product (property) and it shows when you talk about it. If you fixed the house right, the buyer will know what you say is coming from the heart.

Always ask questions and let the buyer respond; for example, "How do you like the kitchen?"
     "I don't really like the color."

46

"We could have it painted before you move in for no charge; it won't costs you a cent, and you could even pick the color. What color do you like?"

"Oh, maybe an off-white."

"That will work nicely. If you want to start today, we can begin right now." Notice that the last sentence is the close. You have the application and lease agreement with you and the tenant also has a copy, which they've been carrying with them. You can now review the contract with the buyer on the kitchen counter or the kitchen table. It is always better to have the tenant sit down as you go through the application and lease agreement.

More About Selling

Becoming professional in everything you do is a lofty goal, and it is a goal you should plan to achieve. You don't have to be an expert salesperson, but you should be professional. And that means acting and behaving in a professional manner. Being professional pays big dividends, and as you progress in your real estate investing, you will come to realize all the benefits that befall the professional. The following are a few things to remember about being professional.

Dress appropriately and be well groomed. Make it a habit to be well groomed and to wear clean clothes. When you are showing your property, you should dress conservatively and like the people who might be buying your house or rental units. Because you are the owner, you should dress smart and be well groomed when you are in front of a buyer. Brian Tracy, in his book, *The Psychology of Selling*, states that 95% of the first impression you make on a person is determined by your clothes. Think about that the next time you prepare to meet a prospective buyer. What will they think of you when they see you?

Be likeable. People rent from people they like. Be pleasant and helpful, courteous and polite—but most of all, be sincere.

Remember your emotions. Buying is emotional. People buy emotionally then think logically about it. Renters are buyers. They want to feel good about what they are buying or renting. This is why you ask how they "feel" about this or that, rather than: "What do you think about this?"

Rehears your knowledge about the property. You should know as much about the property as possible: It is your property isn't it? If you do not know much about it, you should spend time rehearsing questions you will ask a buyer and have the answers to questions the buyers might ask. The twelve most common objections buyers ask are listed later in this chapter. Study your responses to these objections. You need to know how to answer a question before the questions are asked.

What does the renter nee? Give them what they need—then sell them what they want.

Concentrating on value. The value of the property must outweigh its cost. The renter must know she is getting a value from all the benefits the property offers. When you list the rental price, you should set a price that is under the current market by 2% to 10%, especially if you want to get lots of appointments and rent it quickly. If you are in a deflating market—drop the price more. The value the buyer receives will be: (1) A completely updated house or apartment; and (2) the price is listed under market. Make sure your buyer is aware of the exceptional value being offered.

Lower the stress by being a friend. Renting a house or any property can be stressful to most people. It is a large transaction to many, and if they have seen many rentals they can be overwhelmed. To eliminate rental stress, you should be honest, upfront and open with them always. It is better to be a friend rather than someone just trying to rent them a house or apartment.

Property Facts Sheet

This could be a listing printout that makes available all the pertinent information you include about the property. You could also list neighborhood information on the sheet or include it in a package to the buyer. Here is some information you should have available to the buyer:

Location: Explain to the renter the benefits of the location of the property. You could also have a facts sheet of the schools, churches, shopping areas, utility companies, police and fire departments and local government offices.

Upgrades: You should be able to explain in detail all the upgrades to the property and the great amenities that come with it. What are the upgrades, what can they be? Here are a few items that can be categorized as "upgrades."

Interior:

- New Appliances: Stove; range; refrigerator; microwave; dishwasher; clothes washer and dryer.
- New Air Conditioning and heating units.
- New Hot Water Heater.
- New Plumbing fixtures and piping.
- New Electrical wiring and breakers.
- New Sinks bath and kitchen.
- New tile flooring in bath and kitchen and new granite or tiled countertops. Explain the type of tile or granite by name; that would include marble flooring as well.
- New Interior paint.
- Crown moldings and baseboard moldings.
- Ceiling Fans.
- Refinished hardwood floor. You should know the wood type and if it is the original wood flooring. If it is White or Golden oak mention it to the buyer. If it is Maple or Dade County Pine mention it. It is said that Dade County Pine is termite resistant; the little buggers simply don't like the taste of it. And it does make a beautiful wood floor. Most people appreciate a little of the old with the new. And originally restored wood flooring is high on the list.
- New built-ins for ample storage

Exterior:

- New Roof: Asphalt Shingles (15-30 years); Wood Shake (30-50 years);Slate, Concrete and Tile roofs (75-200 years).
- New Sprinkler system for your garden and green yard
- New Paint on house, shutters, and eaves. Explain that the house will not need a paint job for 20 years.
- New Landscaping.
- New concrete or brick driveway.
- New doors and hardware.
- New garage door. New porch light fixture and mailbox.

This will give you an idea of the many items of upgrades you could list. Go through your house and take notes of all the special features of the house, and list them all. And you should be able and willing to talk about them as part of your selling presentation. For instance, you ask the buyer, "Do you like the bathroom?" Then wait for a response.

"Wow. Yes."

"Those are 16 inch Walnut Travertine Marble tiles from Turkey…. It's natural stone. Could you see the expression on your friends faces when you show them the bathroom? Would you like to put in an offer on this house today?" Lead right into a close, every opportunity you have.

Yard: In many areas, backyards are not maintained well. If you spend a little effort on the backyard, it could be a strong selling point to a family that enjoys being outside, playing with dogs and barbequing. The front yard, can again, be a positive selling point. If you've done your job right, the curb appeal of your property is probably the nicest on the street. And if you put in a new picket fence that separates the property from the sidewalk or street, it too is a selling point. It is all the little things that add-up to one nice package.

All the Benefits: What are all the benefits of renting your house compared to other houses for rent in the area? You could write this out on a separate fact sheet for the prospect. Again, let it be known you have all the answers regarding your house. And if you don't know the answer to a particular question, you know where to get it.

Always pay attention to the prospect: The expressions the renter shows and the comments they make to each other will enable you to ask closing questions at the right time. The number one thing to remember is to ask questions that enable you to narrow down objections. Once you know the objections, you can answer the renter's concerns with another closing question. Once you have answered the objections you are on your way to closing the sale.

Use choice words: Never call the lease agreement a contract. It is an *agreement*. People are afraid of contracts. Also, do not tell the prospect to *sign* anything. The word *sign* is intimidating to some. So, instead we use the words *"put your okay here"* or "I just need your *authorization* here."

Twelve Most Common Renter Objections

Many objections renters have are common ones, and you should be able to respond properly to them when they are presented. In this section, I have selected twelve of the most common objections renters have. Study the responses to these objections carefully. And remember, "objections" are nothing more than questions or concerns of the prospective renter.

1. *We want to see more properties before we sign a lease.* You should ask the renters if they like the house/apt. and if it fills their needs. Explain to them that they can okay the lease and still look at other properties, and that you will allow them a contingency period (7 days option) to bailout of the agreement, should they still be uncertain about the lease. You can ask for a deposit of 10 percent of the monthly lease. They can comeback anytime within 7 days and get their money back. After 7 days you keep the deposit. The deposit is used for the first month rent when they move-in.

2. *We would really like an extra bedroom.* You should ask the renter: "Do you really need and extra bedroom?" Then proceed to explain the price difference of rent, one with another bedroom and ask if the renter can afford the difference.

51

3. *The bedroom is small.* If it is only one child's bedroom that is too small, have the renter elaborate by asking this question: "How many children will sleep in this room and do they have a lot of toys?" If they plan to stay in the house/apt. several years, the toys will typically go into the garage for storage or will be discarded. If they have two children for the room, you could suggest using a bunk-bed. If the size of the bedroom is the only issue holding the buyers back from making an offer today, then stay with them until you assure them that the bedroom will suit the needs of their family.

If the master bedroom is in question, shift the focus to the rest of the unit by clarifying the importance of the rest of the house/apt., its location and price. You should always ask direct questions, for example: "Is the size of the master bedroom going to prevent you from signing a lease?" If they say, "maybe," then have them walk through the unit again. "Maybe," means we are almost convinced we want to lease it. Keep them in the house as long as possible until they give you an emphatic "yes" we want to lease, or "no" we don't want it.

4. *The kitchen is small.* You could ask: "Do you do a lot of cooking?" If they respond with a "yes," you simply state that the kitchen is easy to move around in and because of its size, clean-up can be done quickly. If they don't do a lot of cooking, you simply give the same answer: "That's great, there is a lot less to clean: Wouldn't you agree?"

5. *The bathroom is small.* If the buyers are large (stature and/or girth), it could be an issue you may not be able to get around. If it is a secondary bathroom, you could state its minimalist functionality and how quickly it can be cleaned. You could also focus on its European inspired space-saving design. These responses can also be directed to a master bath if needed.

6. *Wish there was another bathroom.* Don't say "Well, how many times do you go to the bathroom?" Or "Do you have a weak bladder?" This is a tough one. Most of the houses/apt. you'll be investing in has one or two bathrooms. Some of the houses/apt. you buy will remain with one bath. Typically, one bath houses are no longer the norm for most families.

Apartments are different. If you are renting a one bath house you have to make sure of three things: (1) the house is in excellent shape; (2) there are many upgrades and special surprises or features in the house; (3) the front and backyards are outstanding.

The renters are usually informed to the number of bathrooms before an appointment is set to show the property. If they know the number of bathrooms and they still want to see the property, then it is not a major objection when they say "Wish there was another bathroom." If it were really important to them, they wouldn't waste the time to come out.

7. *There is no dining room.* If your rental does not have a formal dining room, explain to the renters about using partitions or a room divider; you could also use large potted plants to separate areas. Part of the living area could be separated and made into a dining area. Be creative with renters and show them what can be done.

8. *The yard is small.* Do not agree with the renters by saying, "Yes, it is small." You should emphasize the positive: "Doesn't it feel cozy in this backyard? It's a very low maintenance yard. Wouldn't you agree?" Don't forget to smile.

9. *We would like to show our parents and see what they think.* Ask: "Oh, are your parents going to live with you?" The renters will typically give one of three responses: (1) Yes, they will be living with us; (2) we promised to show them the house before we rent in; (3) they are helping with the rent. Explain to the renters that you could state in the lease that the contract is contingent on the parent's disapproval of what the renters have agreed to. Get the parents on the phone while you are at the house and explain the situation. Then ask if the parents can come over right now. If they live far from the area you'll have to set an appointment. Get the parents and the renters over to the property as soon as possible.

10. *The neighbor's house is really rundown.* This is how you respond to this concern: "That is why I have the rent price on this house priced so competitively. And that is why you will be able to rent this house at a great price—its priced under market." You wrap it up with this: "Did you know

53

the average person moves every seven years? That means that house will probably be up for sale or rent soon and the new owners will definitely fix-up the property.

11. *The rent is too high.* Nearly 100% of the time the renters knew the rent amount before they walked over the threshold. When renters say: "The rent is too high," they are really saying, show me the *value*. All renters, and buyers, everybody wants a deal. You could respond to this objection in three ways: (1) "Can you afford the monthly payments?" (2) "Can you afford the security, first and last month's rent?" (3) "Is it really the price?" If you have qualified the renter before showing the property, you know they *can* afford it. Ask the renter, if he or she were to make an adjustment to the rent rate what would it be? If the renter said $200 below your asking price of $1,500, you should immediately ask: "How close can you come to the asking price?" If renter responds, "that's it," you ask: "Do you really like the house/space, are you happy with it?" If renter says "yes," Now ask the renter: "Can you afford $6.67 a day to share with your family the happiness this house could bring?" Now, that might sound corny, and the renter might even chuckle, but it throws in a low price for happiness. This also may help the renter realize that the price difference may not be worth haggling over if there is a chance of losing the house to another renter.

Explain to the renter that over the term of the lease, the money will make little difference and the renter will get the house he or she wants—the right house for your family.

12. *We would like to think about it before we put in an offer.* Find out what the buyers needs to think about. You could ask: "What concerns do you have about the house?" You have to get the buyers to open-up. Ask questions that will enable you to answer their concerns, such as: "Is the living room large enough? Do you like the paint color?" Keep asking questions until they open up.

Chapter 4

Ancillary Income
Part I

The biggest human temptation is to settle for too little.
—Thomas Merton

Many landlords do not appreciate or fully understand, or simply ignore the importance that ancillary income methods play in the overall cash flow of their rental property. Getting vacant units filled fast is important, and to a degree, anticipating or projecting the ancillary cash flow from future tenants is no less important when it can amount to 5 percent or more of the gross income.

In brief, I am going to introduce you to a few ideas that, as a landlord, you may have not considered. The four ideas here weigh heavily on the aspects of generating income from ancillary sources and how they relate to your prospective tenants. The question that I am going to pose is this: Should you consider projected income from prospective tenants ancillary spending as part of the overall rent when weighing the benefits of future tenants and the number of people on the application, notwithstanding the number of children involved?

If a single man were to rent a two bedroom apartment from you, you would not receive much ancillary income. That is, single men do not do laundry very often and do not generally feed your vending machines as households filled with children would. Retired folks spend even less on ancillary items. But should a family with two children rent the same two bedroom apartment, would you receive more income on a monthly basis than from the single man, even when the apartment rent is the same? Yes. Let us see why. I call this the Ancillary Children System.

The Ancillary Children System

Do more children bring in more cash? When you own apartments and you have a laundry room, soda and snack machines, or video game machines, the answer is most definitely, yes.

Let us examine this situation on a conservative basis. If one of your rental units had a household consisting of three children 12 to 17 in age and each spent $4 per week using your soda and snack machines, you would receive a gross monthly income of $48

And the laundry usage (washer and dryer) with three teen agers could most likely increase to an additional two loads per week or $4 per load, $8 per week total.

Now where do we stand at the end of the month? Well, you've brought in $48 from vending, and a total of $32 ($8 x 4 weeks—loads) from additional laundry usage, for a grand total of $80. Naturally, you will have more water usage and the cost of vending inventory, so we will deduct 40 percent for total cost of goods for a 60 percent net profit of $48. Soda and vending items costs average of $.25 per item and sell for $1.00. Most of the cost associated for our example is from extra water and electricity usage from laundry and water usage from units where the three children live.

In one year the additional net income from the three children would be $576. If rent for the unit is $950 (3/1), your net ancillary income equals, in this case, 5 percent of your rent. If your tenant stays for two or more years, your income will gradually rise when you raise the prices on your laundry and vending machines and increase the amount of rent for your unit.

Consider all possible tenants scenarios and especially tenants with kids. You may have a higher water bill and general wear and tear on the unit, but over the course of the lease, when you have other income related items (laundry, vending, etc.) available, your income will increase substantially. If you have a ten unit building and had five units filled with kids, how much more income would you generate?

Average Laundry Load per Month

The average unit, with two adults will give you about five loads of wash per month. And that would equal the same for the dryer. If you charge $1.75 per wash and $1.75 per dry, then your income should be $3.50 per load; wash and dry. Five loads per month would be $17.50. The monthly gross for four units would be $70. If you are offering cold water wash only your profit after water and electricity cost would be about $50. If you bought new machines at about $600 each, it would take you two years to pay for the machines and make a profit. That is really not that bad, but if you had two to three more people in each unit, then your profit would more than double. For example, we have experienced in two five unit buildings were the average load per unit was over eleven loads per month. This happens when the tenants have young children or when there are many day laborers or working class people in the units. The reason we believe the load rate per month is so high is that most of the tenants work at dirty jobs; their clothes are soiled to extreme and the fact that they do not have a lot of clothes to wear means they must wash their clothes more often. A tenant who must do a lot of laundry to clean the few articles of clothing they have, though sad as it might be, is good for you and your cash flow.

Here you will find a guideline of how far you can get with one washer and one dryer according to the Multi-family Housing Association:

- *Families*: One washer/dryer pair per 7 to 12 units.

- Yo*ung Working Adults*: One pair per 7 to 20 units.

- *Older Working Adults*: One pair per 12 to 20 units

- *Students*: One pair per 20 to 40 students

- *Seniors*: One pair per 20 to 45 units

As you can see, you do not need a lot of machines to do the job. One washer/dryer pair can handle many single tenants and families. Do not think about adding more machines until you have 30 or 40 people, 2-3 bedroom units and where most of your tenants are families. Students and seniors do not do as many loads as young working adults and families with young children

More People—More Ancillary Income

Here are a few things to consider:

- Two people in a one bedroom apartment will generate more income from laundry and vending machines than a single tenant—in most cases.

- Households with children will always generate higher ancillary income.

- A couple with a baby will always generate more ancillary income.

- Seniors generate the lowest ancillary income as a group

- Blue collar workers generate the highest next to teenagers as income for ancillary products

- Laborers and day laborers are among the highest spenders for laundry and vending machines.

Educated, white collar tenants are among the lowest cash generators for ancillary products when considering vending machines.

Price Adjustments For Amenities Offered

Certain amenities offered in your rental property can increase your monthly cash flow and add significant value to your building over the long-term. We've listed below some amenities a rental could have and an estimate of the value-added rental premium for such amenity. The premiums we list below are averages we have added to rentals which we have used to increase the monthly rental price.

You should frequently make it a habit to compare your units with others in your area. If your units offer more and better amenities, then, adjust your rental price to reflect the differences; and make certain to emphasize the difference in your advertisement as well, and when you show the unit to the prospective tenant. It is important to explain your amenities especially when you know your competition does not have what you are offering. All special or unique characteristics of a unit should be brought to the potential tenants attention.

Amenities in Unit	Approximate Monthly Premium You should charge
Air Conditioning Wall Unit	$20-25
Central Air Conditioning	$35-60
Cable T.V. Paid	$50-65
Dishwasher	$10-15
Disposal	$ 0-5
Fireplace	$10-15
Mirrored Closets	$10-15
Larger closets or Walk-in closet	$10-15
Refrigerator	$30-40
Storage facility	$20-30
Utilities Paid	$30-40
Washer and Dryer Connection	$40-50
Washer and Dryer Included	$75-80

Building Amenities

Balcony or Patio	$20-30
Business Center	$ 5-10
Carport Parking	$25-30
Private Garage	$75-80
Parking Garage	$25-30

Exercise Room	$10-15
Secured Building	$50-65
Laundry Room	$10-15
Recreation Room	$10-15
Swimming Pool and Spa	$10-15
Sports Courts	$ 0-5

If there are items missing from this list that you have in your unit or on your property, go ahead and compare it to the closes item on the from and use your best judgment to place a value on it.

Look over your property inside and out, and determine what extra amenities are you offering tenants. What do you believe the amenity is worth in monthly rental income? Is it something the potential tenant can benefit from? If so, it is definitely worth a value.

What is Cash Flow?

I want to do a little backtracking here. The aim of holding property and renting it is to make money. There should be no other reason you should want to hold property. You are in it for mainly two types of benefits: (1) appreciation; and (2) Cash flow or positive income.

Cash flow is the cash left over after you have collected all the rents and other income associated with your property and paid all the operating expenses and mortgage payments. Cash flow is typically referred to as *positive cash flow*; this means, you have a positive cash income each month or year after all operating expenses (property taxes, insurance, utility bills, property maintenance, and so on) and mortgage payments.

When you have negative cash flow, you are losing money monthly or yearly; your investment is not producing enough actual cash to support itself, and therefore, you are forced to pay the expenses of your property by bringing in more outside funds. This may not be all bad for your investment; you still have many tax benefits, including depreciation and perhaps the property is in an area with strong appreciation that may offset your loses. But, relying on appreciation and tax benefits is not a sound investment strategy. The negative cash flow problem must be conquered for you to truly succeed in the long-term. And you should make every effort of find and execute ways that allow you to increase your monthly and annual cash flow.

As investment properties become more and more expensive, it becomes exceedingly difficult to become cash flow positive; you must think of ways to increase the income from your properties, so that they are self-supporting and they do not need recurring cash infusions to remain as a going concern.

There are many creative ways to produce income from owning rental property; collecting rents is only one way. We have, over the years, increased cash flow significantly incorporating the techniques and strategies included in this book. And we hope this book will empower you to think more creatively and possibly even come up with new ideas of income generation yourself.

How Do You Get Positive Cash Flow from Your Rentals?

Most apartments operating expenses run about 45%-50% of gross income and rental houses run about 20%, then how do you capture positive cash flow with a low capitalization rate?

There are four ways:

- Buy fixers or handyman specials at a 30% or greater discount to the market. Make necessary repairs and increase rents.

- Your loan to value ratio is low; you put up a 40% or higher down payment.

- Increase the value of your property in every way possible, then increase rents.

- Create other sources of income from the property. Add a coin-op laundry or collect a $50 application fee opposed to a $20 one.

The cash flow strategies in this section will either save you money or make you a lot of money. Many of the ideas presented here will increase the value of your property and create for you the best chances of securing positive cash flow on all your rental properties.

Other Ancillary Income Ideas You May Want to Consider

This is a concise list of income increasing ideas that I have used to force appreciation on property, but also to increase the monthly cash flow. When you are looking at a property to buy or your current rental(s), you must use your imagination with the space you have. Could you add another bedroom by erecting a wall, yet without adding more square footage? Could you turn an attic or basement into a livable rental unit? I have, and they have worked out great. Could you rent a garage separately for $200 a month as storage space?

Here are more ideas:

- Create two rentable units from one (did this)
- Turn garage into an efficiency rental (did this)
- Rent rooms separately (did this)
- Rent by the head (did this)
- Sell signage (You could also sell sign space the side of your building if you are on a busy street)
- Charge more for large families (did this)
- Go to Special Agencies that Might Pay Higher Rents (did this)
- Rent furniture and Appliances (did this)
- Build more units on larger lots (Multi-family zoning) (did this)
- Offer upgrades (did this) This is covered in Chapter 5 Part II
- Charge an Application Fee (charge more) (did this)
- Charge a Satellite Fee (did this)
- Charge a Pet Fee (monthly) (did this)
- Charge Late Rent Fee (did this)

- Charge for Lawn and Landscaping Maintenance (for houses) (did this)
- Charging for credit card, PayPal and Square transaction (5%)

Establish Renters Insurance

Most renters do not have renters insurance. This is good. It allows you the opportunity to either sell them a policy or sell them a renter's insurance service—a service which you offer to your tenants at the time the lease is signed. The difference between selling a policy and offering a service will be defined as you read on.

First, "What is renters insurance?" Renters insurance is coverage for personal property, such as a T.V., sound system, furniture, jewelry, collectible items, etc.; anything the tenant values. Personal items are not covered by the landlords property insurance. Renters insurance is for anyone who rents or leases residential space and the coverage is usually for theft or damages to personal property.

A specific policy could cover damages by:

- Theft
- Fire or lightning
- Vandalism or Malicious Mischief
- Windstorm
- Water damage

A renters policy can also provide liability protection, such as:

- Unintentional bodily injury to you and others on your property.

- Liability protection against accidents that occur on your property.

- Payments for medical bills for people visiting you and get hurt. For example, a friend trips over your sofa and breaks his arm, would be covered under your renter's insurance policy.

How Can You Make Money with Renters Insurance?

There are three ways to make money with renters insurance:

1) If you are a licensed insurance agent you could sell your tenant's renters insurance along with auto, health, life and everything else.

2. Contact a licensed insurance agent; a friend or relative would be nice. Sign a referral fee agreement. Make an introduction to your tenant who is interested in insurance. A $20 or $25 referral fee from the agent in fair, but it is completely negotiable. A better way is to ask the insurance agent what he makes on the policy and negotiate a 10 percent finder's fee or referral fee that is ongoing; even if the tenant moves from your rental to another building. As long as the tenant uses the same insurance agent you should receive a fee. If the tenant uses the same insurance agent for five years you could receive a check from the agent ones a month over the five year period. This could be a substantial amount if you were to have many tenants sign up for insurance. For instance, if twenty tenants get insurance and on a monthly bases you receive $5 monthly referral fee you would receive $100 a monthly, which would be $1,200 per year and $6,000 for five years.

3. The third way to increase your cash flow is to offer a renters insurance service. The service is offered when the new tenant signs the lease. The renter's insurance agreement is attached to the back of the lease. If they do not sign it then, contact them every few months in the form of a personal letter (See figure 1, Renters Insurance Service Letter) then followed by a phone call. The service is offered by the property manager which is you or your assistant. What is the service? It's very simple; first explain what renters insurance is and what it covers; for instance, Renters Insurance is coverage for personal property for anyone who rents or leases space. The

personal property (T.V., furniture, jewelry, etc.) is covered from theft and damage.

Next: For a fee, let's use $49 for this example; you will complete the following service for the tenant.

1) Contact a licensed insurance company.
2) Handle all the paperwork.
3) Negotiate for the lowest quote possible on your behalf.
4) The tenant will receive a stress-free transaction and he   will maintain the security   and peace of mind knowing all   of their valued possessions are insured.

The Best Solution

The best situation would entail you to combine the referral fee and the service agreement. This would allow you to reap the highest cash return.

Example: If you signed-up ten tenants with a service fee of $49 each and   received a flat referral fee of $25 per tenant from the insurance agent you would receive a total of $740. If you decided to take the 10 percent finder's fee in a way described earlier, you could receive an additional $50 monthly ($5 per person). This amount could be paid to you indefinitely until the policy is cancelled.

You may charge whatever you what for a service fee. The fee should be at a price that is affordable to most of your tenants and at the same time high enough to make it worthwhile for you.

There is some work involved here, but with some organization; introducing renters insurance to your tenants could be well worth your time.

Summing Up

Ancillary income could add significant cash flow to your overall rental. The cost associated with installation of laundry and vending machines can usually be recovered in less than twelve months. Do not believe landlords who say that you cannot make money with these types of machines. They are wrong. If you work it like a business you will make money—and lots of it.

Always consider the number of people moving into a unit. If you sign a long-term lease (2-5 years), you could add greater cash flow when you rent to a family. A single tenant rarely ever spends more on your machines than a family of four, five or six. Keep this in mind.

Think of the long-term cash you will generate with ancillary income. If you make $120 a month profit from a Pepsi machine, it may not tickle your money bone; but as a long-term in investor, a ten year span will give you extra $14,400 cash, for a business that is completely passive. You may have to spend about an hour a month filling sodas and collecting coins.

Owning good rental property is about controlling good cash flow—cash flow from multiple sources. Do not limit yourself to just rental income. Offer your tenants services and products for a price and let them tell you if they like it, want it and need it. If you do not get the ancillary income, the money will go somewhere else.

Chapter 5

Ancillary Income
Part II

Offering Upgrades

A clever real estate investor learns to create multiple income opportunities.

When you are in the process of signing a lease with a new tenant you should have what is referred to as an *upgrade list*. This list will contain a number of upgrades to the rental unit which management will install or perform for an additional fee. Like a trained monkey, dancing to the beat of the organ grinder, management will perform almost anything for a fee. There are numerous upgrades and services you (your assistant, team member or handyman), could perform, that could increase your cash flow (beyond the rent), every time you sign-up a tenant on a new lease.

Sample Upgrades

Offering upgrades also secures the tenant for a longer term occupancy by getting them actively involved with the apartment or rental unit with personal touches.

- *Paint.* You could offer a different color paint for the unit or have the tenant bring in their own colors.

- *Upgraded Appliances.* Refrigerator, stove, etc.

- *Installation of a ceiling fan.* If one does not already exist, you could offer this service.

- *Door peephole.* If the entrance door does not have a peephole, you could put one in for the tenant.

- *Carpet.* If the current carpet is not agreeable to the tenants' tastes, you could place a new one in the unit to the tenants' liking.

- *Mini-blinds.* If the tenant wants different mini-blinds or simply a different color, you could offer different varieties of blinds or even different types of window coverings.

- *Air Conditioner.* If the tenant wants a larger window air conditioner, you could charge an extra $15 per month, and include another $40 installation charge.

As you can see there is a host of upgrades you could offer. The standard upgrades mentioned above will be a course of discussion as we move forward in this chapter and I will present a detailed plan for each upgrade starting with upgraded paint color.

Paint

All of your rental units should be painted the same color. Usually, the color is a earthy, off-white or light shade of yellow. Country White and Antique White by Color Place can be bought right off the shelf from Wal-Mart. Light shades of grey can also be used to offset white trim. Almost all large real estate companies paint the interior walls these colors, and so should you. Off-white walls and white ceilings are pleasing to most people. And wood trim, door casing, baseboards, and crown-moldings are nearly always painted white. White makes a place look clean, bright and it is easy to replace when one needs to repaint.

If you decide to offer a paint-option to your new tenant and your new tenant is willing to pay for the paint, brushes and all other materials, including labor, then you must first specify a color, what room or rooms are to be painted. And then you'll need to set a time to start and a time when the painting is finished, and finally, when the tenant can begin to move in furniture and other personal items.

You will need to get an estimated time frame as to the length of time it will take to paint and complete the project. Since you won't be doing the painting yourself, you will take the position as the manager of the project and hire the individuals to do the job. Your handyman, if you have one, could be the perfect choice.

The following is a sampling of what you may want to charge; but keep in mind of your costs, materials, labor and so on. A realistic price to the tenant could be 10 percent to 20 percent over your costs. If labor and materials costs a total of $500, then you could reasonably charge the tenant $600 to $700 for the project. Your profit would be $100 to $200 dollars. If you have lots of time on your hands and enjoy painting, you could do the work yourself and make a profit of $500 or more for a day or two of painting.

One room (bedroom): Most bedrooms can be painted in less than one day and with all materials, including paint, and labor costs less than $150. The labor is the most expensive cash outlay, so, it is critical to curb the labor cost at all times. You can charge about $200 or a little less depending on your labor costs per bedroom. If you are in a high rent area, then by all means, you should charge more, perhaps $250-$350 per bedroom.

Two Rooms (bedroom (2) or living room): A charge of $400 to $500 is reasonable. This includes, interior window frames, if requested, floor boards, door casings and other moldings, along with crown moldings.

Bath only: $150 to $200 is a reasonable estimate.

Kitchen only: Around $150 to $300 depending on size.

The whole place: This could range over $2,000 for an entire house of 1,000 sq. ft., and a lot more depending on size. You might want to call a couple of painting contractors and have each give you a quote on painting the interior of a house and/or individual rooms. This will enable you to breakdown the hourly charge and allow you the information you need to charge a realistic price to your tenant.

Most painting contractors overcharge based on an hourly rate. You might be shocked at some of the quotes you receive from painting contractors. Most are highly overpaid for their service, and this is the reason why many small time landlords choose to do their own painting.

If you use an individual with some painting experience, you can pay between $120 to $150 per day. In an eight hour work day that would range from $15 to $18.75 per hour. You shouldn't be in a position to pay anymore than this for interior painting. For a professional painter, you can go up to $25 per hour. They will typically work a bit faster and the quality of work will be better and expenses for materials possibly less. Do keep track of time. Some contractors will pace themselves for the entire eight hour day when the work to be completed is no more than a four or five hour job.

Appliances

There are two ways to offer appliance upgrades: (1) when you acquire more expensive appliances in rental houses or apartments, or purchase them at deep discounted prices from closeouts, going out of business sales, people who need to get rid of fairly new appliances to raise cash, or from any numerous sources, do not place these top of the line appliances in your rental units. Store them in your garage or other storage space somewhere and offer them to your tenants as upgrades.

Refrigerator. A basic refrigerator in a rental house or apartment should cost no more than $350 to $500 brand new. Used refrigerators in good condition in and out should cost between $50 to $300. A refrigerator should last well over ten years. If you've acquired a $1,500 refrigerator for $300, do not immediately place it in the unit. This type of refrigerator is worth an extra $10 to $20 per month. And you can get this amount and more when you offer it in your *Appliance Upgrade Package.*

The extra $15 to $20 per month may not sound like much, but at the end of the year you just made $180 to $240 more had you not offered the upgrade. You have also allowed a tenant who has never or could never had the opportunity to have a $1,500 refrigerator at her disposal. Most of your tenants could never afford to purchase a top of the line refrigerator that costs $1,500 or $2,500. So when you have the opportunity to buy one the $200 or $300, make the commitment and offer it as an upgrade.

Stove/Range. Stoves come in all styles, sizes and prices. Ranging from less than $200 to several thousands of dollars, upgrading a stove can be a high profit margin item, when the tenant is an avid cook and can appreciate the usage of a good top of the line stove. Now, I'm not talking about a chef stove that can cost several thousands of dollar; this would make little sense from a business standpoint, but a $500 stove is a very nice stove with all the gadgets an avid cook could appreciate. Receiving $15 to $20 per month for this type of stove is not unreasonable.

Microwave. Sometimes you can get deals on stoves with a matching overhead microwave. These are typically larger microwaves with more power and faster heating times. The new GE microwaves costs about $200 to $240. If you are to offer this type of microwave, or more expensive ones, you should expect to charge your tenant $10 to $15 per month as an upgraded item. At $10 per month, you will have received your cash investment back within two years.

Microwaves that costs $30 to $100 new, can be leased out at $5 to $10 per month as an upgraded item. Many smaller C and D class apartments do not provide tenants with microwaves; this is usually the responsibility of the tenant, and most landlords leave it at that. But if you are serious about increasing your rental business cash flow, take a serious look into offering not just microwaves, but all appliances as an upgraded item.

Dishwasher. Not all apartments, or homes for that matter, have

73

dishwashers. Most homes or apartments built forty years ago did not come with, and where not designed for a dishwasher in the kitchen. If you do have units with dishwashers, add an updated dishwasher charge of $10 per month for the unit. If your unit does not have a dishwasher in it, but your tenants would like one and even pay your monthly fee, then you'll have to work out the numbers. Here are a few things to consider before you jump in with a dishwasher:

- Does the kitchen have space for it?
- Usually, a dishwasher is near the sink. Is there room there for it?
- Who will breakout the cabinet? Will it fit under the counter?
- Who will do the plumbing connection?
- If you are not going to do the work, get a quote from three plumbers regarding installation.
- Older apartments and homes may not have the electrical capacity to run the dishwasher; therefore, check your amps. A large microwave might need extra power as well.

If your dishwasher costs $250 (lower range) you could also spend $100 to $250 on the installation--so, keep this in mind. Figure in your profit and how long it will take you to get your cash investment back. Another thing you should consider with a dishwasher is the extra water expense. If you pay for the water bill from your rental units, a dishwasher uses a lot more water than washing dishes by hand. It is guaranteed your water bill will increase. Keep track of your higher water expense. You may even want to raise a dishwasher upgrade charge to $25 to $30 per month. When your rental unit already comes with a dishwasher make certain to increase the rental rate with this in effect.

Clothes Washer and Dryer. Rental houses have washer and dryer hookups, unlike many older apartments. Offering washer and dryer upgrade leasing is good business for many landlords. Studies have shown that the average tenant does seven loads of laundry per month. When using coin operated machines at a Laundromat the typical individual will spend $24.50 per month doing laundry or about $3.50 per load, wash and dry. This does not include detergent expense, travel time and gas expense to and from the Laundromat. Therefore, by offering a washer and dryer to your tenant may

74

be a welcomed relief.

Plan to invest no more than $400 for each new machine. If you could find new ones for $300 to $350, even better. Look into special holiday sales for bigger discounts. Natural gas dryers cost a little more, but may save the tenant a little on their monthly energy bill.

If you charged a $30 monthly fee for the machines, it would take you twenty-six months to recoup your investment if you paid $400 per machine and fewer than two years when you've invested $300 per machine. After two or three years your positive cash flow is about $360 per year. And if you raise your lease rate to $40 per month, you are up to $480 per year on extra cash flow.

Remember, washers use a lot of water, so, make sure the tenant is the one paying the water bill.

Sell the washer/dryer lease package at the time of signing the rental lease. The benefit to the tenants is twofold: (1) if they cannot afford a new washer and dryer, they now have it available to them; and (2) they are able to enjoy the convenience of never having to hop in the car and go to the Laundromat.

Repairs to Appliances

You should state in your appliance lease agreement that all repairs are the responsibility of the tenant not the landlord. And make sure your tenant is aware of the condition of the machines: "They are new or nearly new and have a life span of over ten years." You should also make sure to get sufficient security deposits and credit card information during the lease signing. This is important in case your tenant has a lapse in memory and loads the machines in a truck when they move.

Another Outlet for Expensive Appliances

Instead of placing expensive appliances in rental units, consider selling them and try to buy two new, apartment quality ones for the price of the one you sell. For example: I had purchased a three unit building that an investor had given up on, for any number of reasons. Inside each of the kitchens was a brand new stainless steel, 20 cubic feet, bottom freezer refrigerator worth $1,900 on the low end; stove/range $500, over the stove microwave $250 and a dishwasher, $300. There were three of each appliances in each unit. The two, one bedroom apartments did not really need dishwashers, but since they were already built in, it would be easier to raise the rent a few bucks more than to remove and repair the cabinets.

Ceiling Fan

Ceiling fans ranging in price from $20 to $40 are your best bet and can be purchased at most home improvement stores or Wal-Mart. When a tenant is willing to pay a service charge for a ceiling fan upgrade the fan remains with the unit long after the tenant leaves. If there is a light fixture in the living room and one in the bedroom, and after showing the tenant a brochure with the two or three styles of fans available, and wishes to have one purchased and installed, you can do the work easily and have it installed in less than an hour after purchase.

You can charge an hourly rate above what you charge your installer or $25 per hour for installation. Add another 20 percent to the materials used and price of the fan. You won't make much on this offering, $20 or $30, but you do get a free fan out of it and that is an upgrade to the next tenant and it also increases the attractiveness and value to the unit.

Door Peephole

Many older apartments and houses do not have peepholes. Installing a peephole in the front entrance door is easy and can be completed in about fifteen minutes, provided you have a drill and a peephole on hand. A good thing about a peephole, is that it remains in the door after the tenant leaves.

If you have older apartments, you can sell this service as part of a upgrade at the time of the lease signing. Show a picture in the brochure, and explain the security and safety measure of a peephole.

Peepholes can be purchased at most hardware stores for under $5 and you can charge $25 to have it installed. All it takes is to drill a small hole in the door at eye level, or lower for children to use. Once the hole is drilled, insert the peephole. Anyone can do this, and it is a quick and easy money maker, that stresses safety and security.

Carpet

Some tenants prefer wall to wall carpet rather than bare hardwood floors. In colder regions of the U.S. and Canada carpet is preferred by many tenants for its warmth and insulation. In the southern states, with higher year round temperatures and humidity, it is less desirable.

Carpeting in rental properties is usually a waste of money over the long-term, because it can be ruined easily by humans and pets. And when a large stain cannot be removed, you may have to replace the carpet in the entire room. Some carpets have a half of holding on to unpleasant odors even after a few steam cleanings. The point here is, not to spend too much money on carpet even if it is an upgrade and our tenant will pay for it and installation. Your tenant may be a tenant for only a year and after that, you may have to ripe it out if it wasn't care for well or it is an unpleasant color most tenants may not agree with.

Try to stay with average quality carpet that costs under a $1 per square foot. Preferably $.50 to $.75 per square foot is better. You can get this type of carpet immediately from Lowe's or Home Depot and have it cut and installed the same day. At the back of these two stores you'll find the rolls available to choose from. No need to order a custom carpet that takes weeks to arrive--you need to have the job completed within a day or two. You can buy a number of the swatches there for about 50 cents each and you can place them on a piece of clean cardboard or a thin piece of wood and show it as your selection of sample carpets; just like at the carpet stores.

You could also try a few for the local carpet retailer in your area. Discounters are great for blowout prices, but they may not carry the same carpet a few month from the time you collect your sample set of carpet swatches. You need to shop at a reliable store that will always have your carpets styles and colors available.

The easiest way to figure out what to charge and then what you'll make is to add up your costs: labor, carpet, materials (tact's, staples or carpet gun, adhesive, trowel, utility knife and blades, etc.) and time spent shopping; then include your 20 percent on top for managing the project. Half of estimated payment should be at the signing of the rental lease agreement and the remaining balance at the completion of the project.

Example of a carpet installation charge for tenant and determining price:

One Room: A room 100 square feet with carpet and padding at $1 per square foot will cost $100. That's simple enough. You will need adhesive (glue) that will cost $40 to $50 for a five***** gallon can. Or you can use tact for a wood floor. Add in your labor charge of about $150 and you are at a cost of $250 plus 20 percent ($50) and you have a price for the tenant at $300. If you believe you can get more for your service then charge it. The carpet price and the glue price could be cut in half.

Mini-Blinds

Some of your tenants may prefer mini-blinds to drapes or upgraded blinds as opposed to the ones you offer with the apartment or house. Blinds can get expensive especially when there are lots of windows in the unit. Prices can range from $4 to $5 or inexpensive 1" vinyl blinds to $40 to $60 for 2" wood blinds and about half that price for the wood faux blinds. An easy way to assess the "blind" situation would be to take photos of the blinds and your local Lowe's or Home Depot the next time you go there. Many samples are already hanging. Once the photo is taken jot down the price. You could also go online and to either store and type in "mini blinds"--photos and prices show. You could use the photos in your selling brochure.

Do not bother with custom orders that may take days or weeks before they're available. You want common stock items that can be purchase quickly at all stores.

Again, add 10 percent to 20 percent of the total costs and labor to the price and you have a quote for your tenant.

Air Conditioner

Window Box Air Conditioner. Upgrading to a larger window air conditioner is welcoming luxury in warm weather areas. Other tenants may want more air conditions as well as larger ones. Prices range from $100 to $600 depending on size and BTUs. Here is the break down on prices and power:

- A $100 machine (5,000 BTU) is sufficient for a 100 square foot bedroom.

- A 10,000 BTU machine is good for a room 450 square feet and costs $200.

- A 18,000 BTU is sufficient for a larger room of up to 1,000 square feet and can cost between $350 to $600.

- A 24,500 BTU air conditioner by LG Electronics can cool 1,600 square feet and costs under $400. It also has an Energy Star efficiency rating of 9.4.

Your brochure can offer four models with varying BTU capacity and prices can start at $10 per month for the smaller, $100 machines and up to $40 per month for the larger ones. You should plan to recoup your investment within twelve months. In hot weather regions, your tenants will be glad they upgraded.

Central Air Conditioning. When a tenant asks about central air conditioning, tell them it will cost them $4,000. That will usually shut them up.

Insurance on Appliances

It is worth noting that you may also sell insurance on the appliance upgrades. Since the tenant is liable for all repairs, you might as well include an appliance insurance package for $15 to $30 per month. This way the repairs and the costs of them do not fall on the tenant. While most if not all your appliances will be new or near new, the probability of repairs within the first couple of years should be nil. If you receive, for example, $20 per month as insurance premiums on your own machines, this equates to $240 at the end of the year and that is a nice chuck of change and would certainly pay for damage to a machine that is not the cause of the tenant.

Your insurance offered is a based more on a warranty bases due to faulty manufacturing, not tenant misuse. This will be in the insurance contract.

What Are the Advantages to The Landlord?

The advantages to the landlord are greater than you might expect. Here's the short list:

1. *Everything stays*. Upgraded items all stay with the unit when the tenant moves out. Carpet, Appliances, ceiling fans and all other upgrades to the unit remain. Since the tenant paid you for the items and you get to keep them, it is well worth adding an upgrade service for your tenants.

2. *Other Tenants Become Aware of the Upgrades*. A really nicely upgraded unit can be presented as a model to other future tenants and even current tenants. Some tenants have limited imagination and are unaware of the choices they have or what is available. By having them see an upgraded unit, they may choose to upgrade themselves.

3. *Longer Lease*. Typically, a tenant who pays for the upgrades may plan to stay longer in the unit than just one year. Try for a three year lease if the tenant chooses to do many upgrades. If the tenant is very comfortable with the upgrades, then lock them in for a longer-term lease.

4. *More Money Upfront*. Upgrades allow you, the landlord to get more money upfront. This of course helps with cash flow and brings in a lot more than what would typically come in from collecting rent.

5. *Easier to Rent*. It is easier to rent when a prospective tenant can choose a carpet, paint color or other items to personalize their new home.

They have a choice and the rental becomes a part of them and there own personal style.

6. *Easier to Rent for the Next Tenant.* It might be much easier to rent to the next tenant when the unit has been upgraded. Since everything stays with the unit and the upgrades are in good condition, a prospective tenant will be able to recognize the all the extras. It is a big bonus for the next tenant.

7. *Higher Rent for the Next Tenant.* Of course, with all the upgrades, you will be able to offer the unit at a higher rental rate than the other non-upgraded units. And depending on the upgrades, you could receive anywhere from $25 to $200 more per month. Figure the costs of the upgrades and break it down over the term of the lease. This could give you an idea of what to charge. For instance: If the upgrade costs $600, you could divide that out into a 12 month lease and have the new tenant pay $50 more per month compared to the other units of comparable size.

8. *Quality of Tenant.* With better looking units and extra amenities, you may attract a higher quality of tenants. Like all products being sold, one usually get what one pays for; therefore, with an exceptionally nicely upgraded unit, you may get a higher quality of tenant who is willing and able to pay the extra costs associated with an upgraded unit.

9. *Creates Value.* Like all businesses, rental property is valued based on the income it produces. When you are getting higher rents, you are thereby creating value to the property; you are increasing cash flow and forcing appreciation.

How Much Can You Make?

The increase in cash flow can be quite arbitrary and can range from $10 more per month to several hundred or thousands depending on the size and scope of your operation and the number of units you have.

An easier way to figure out your potential increase in cash flow, provided you offer many of the upgrades as introduced above, is to calculate a certain percentage of interested tenants and then take the average dollar increase per tenant income generated; for instance, after one year of offering twenty tenants the upgrade packages or individual items, seven tenants ended up spending an additional $30 per month and another $1,480 for the year on upgrading paint and other things. $30 per month is $360 per year, multiplied by seven tenants is $2,520, plus $480, and you have now increased your cash flow $4,000. If your average rental apartment leases for $700 per month, twenty units is $14,000 per month and $168,000 per year. By offering an upgrade service you've made an extra $4,000, and increase your total cash flow by 2.4 percent of total rents collected. This is a very realistic example and you should do much better if you decide to focus your energy on consistently offering your *special upgraded service*.

You could use the same agreement used for leasing furniture and appliances. "Furniture Lease Form and Upgrades." 2page contract with upgrades and stipulation that everything must stay with the unit.

Summing Up

Smart landlords use creative ideas to increase cash flow. A great way to improve income is to offer tenants upgrades. Many tenants will want to upgrade something in the unit. Offer tenants multiple upgrade options and you will soon realize healthier monthly cash flow.

Chapter 6

Ancillary Income
Part III
Pet Fees

*All pets are welcome. We never had a pet who smoked in bed and set
fire to the building. We never had to evict a pet because it had drug problems.
We never had a pet who played music too loud or partied through the early
morning. We never had a pet get drunk and put holes in the walls and break all
the windows. We never had a pet leave the gas oven door open to heat the
room. If your pet can vouch for you, you're more than welcome.*

N early 50% of all people have pets. Thus, it can be said that perhaps
50% of all tenants that live in apartments or rental houses will have
a pet. As a landlord you should be thinking of ways to increase
your cash flow by offering your tenants the opportunity to have a pet or pets.
A sad, but true fact reported by the Humane Society has 25% of pets ending
up in shelters are from owners who cannot find suitable rental housing
where pets are allowed. And a very small fraction of those animals ever find
new homes. Most pets are not harmful to the property and most are

moderately behaved and do not cause annoyances to other tenants. Pets have been proven to calm most people and people with pets are likely to rent from you for a longer period than those who do not have pets. However, pets can cause problems; that is remedied by charging an extra deposit and monthly pet rent. The monthly pet rent can increase your cash flow significantly and increase the value of your building. As you read through this chapter, we think you will come to the conclusion that pets are good for your business and you should consider accepting pets if you do not already.

Do You Need a Pet Agreement?

Yes, any tenant who wishes to have a pet should first complete a pet agreement or application (an agreement is enclosed at the end of the chapter). The agreement will state all the conditions that are applicable for providing a healthy home and good care for a pet. The Agreement will also include the monthly fee and extra security deposit, not to mention the general pet policy. Take a photo of the pet and staple it to the Agreement. This will help to identify the animal if it is lost or roaming the building without its owner.

How Much Should The Pet Fee Be?

The pet fee is based on the probable damage a pet can cause. It is also based on what you believe is the highest amount you could possibly charge without it appearing to be excessive. Use the following as a guideline:

- Dogs: small or large $35-$50 per month per dog.
- Cats: $35 per month for one cat and $15 more for second cat.
- Birds: Caged birds $15. Loose bird, (Parrot) $20.
- Rats, Mice, Hamsters, Guinea pig, and Gerbils: $5 per cage per month.
- Snake: $5 caged per month.
- Fish: $10 per month for a 10 to 55 gallon tank. Goldfish bowl is free.

This should give you an idea as to what you can charge. Every situation is different and you must use your own discretion.

84

How Many Pets Per Apartment or House Should Be Allowed?

Two medium sized dogs for a small apartment is enough and probably no more than two dogs per house. Some people accumulate pets like others accumulate shoes. Be strict on the number of pets your tenants want. Many times, after they realize the time and money a pet consumes, they will find another home for their little friend. Every situation is different, so use some common sense.

What Pets Should Not Be Allowed?

Very large dogs that have a natural tendency for aggressive and dangerous behavior should not be allowed; and they include:

- Pit Bulls
- Rottweiler's
- Akita's
- Alaskan Malamutes
- Chow Chows
- Doberman Pinschers
- Siberian Huskies
- Perro de Presa Canarios
- Boxers
- American Staffordshire Terriers
- Great Danes
- Wolf-hybrids
- Any dog that is a mix of any of the above breeds.

There are reportedly 4.7 million dog bites each year in the U.S. And 264 people died from 1982 to 2006 from dog attacks; over 50% were caused by Pitt Bulls and Rottweiler's.

Because of the high liability claims filed with dog bites, insurance companies have blacklisted certain breeds that have shown a pattern of attacks. Your home owners policy or rental property policy may not cover such claims. It is best to never accept the aforementioned aggressive dog breeds.

Now, if the tenant is willing to pay an extra large deposit and an unusually high monthly rent for the dog, then use your discretion. Do give stern warnings about the dogs characteristic behavior patterns and let the owner know, that upon any incident, the animal will have to go. Have the tenant sign an agreement to stipulate these facts.

Other pets that should not be allowed include:

- *Farm animals*: Chickens, roosters, goats, pigs and so on. Of course, if you are renting out a farm or property where current zoning allows for these animals then it would be okay.

- *Uncommon pets*: Monkeys, and/or other endangered or undomesticated animals that belong in the wild. And ladies, your husband is not a big Ape, he could stay.

What Kinds of Pets Should Not Be Charged?

There are some pets you do not charge a fee.

Seeing eye dog for the blind.
A care-giving dog or other pet for a severely handicapped person.
A bowl of goldfish or other fish.

Problems With Dogs?

Who doesn't love dogs? A survey by the American Pet Products Manufacturers Association found that 39% of U.S. households own at least one dog. But, we also know that of all the domesticated pets, dogs have a predisposition of causing damage. Puppies, in particular, urinate on floors, scratch doors, wood trim and cupboards. Dogs, also, if not comfortable with being left alone will whine and bark and cause mischief. If you are renting houses, dogs will ruin back lawns with holes (some dogs love to dig), wood gates with scratches or heavy chewing marks, backdoors that get thrashed, and if the pet owner is lazy, a large mess of dog doo in the yard. Make sure you charge enough for large dogs and make sure you collect a sizable security deposit. An additional security deposit of $250-$500 is reasonable for a large dog. Double the security deposit for each dog if there is more than one.

Deposit For Each Pet?

It is a good idea to collect a deposit for each pet. If a tenant has a dog and a cat, take two deposits; $250 for the dog and $100 for the cat. If a tenant has two large dogs at you rental house, take two larger deposits; $250 for one dog and another $250 for the other. Stick to your policy. The owner of the animals will tell you that the dogs are peaceful; "they do not, scratch, bite or dip holes". Do not waver on your deposits or your pet fee.

How Much More Can You Really Make by Charging a Pet Fee?

The money you make will increase your cash flow by more than you think. With one dog, a fee of $35 per month is $420 per year. If you own an apartment with eight rental units and 50% of your tenants have a small dog, your monthly cash flow would improve $140 ($35 for each of the four dogs per month), or $1,680 for 12 months. And if you have a 16 unit building and half of your tenants have a dog, you would improve your monthly income by $280, or $3.360 in the course of a year.

Because your income has increase by renting to people with pets, you have also increased the value of your property. If your building is in an area where the average Gross Rent Multiplier is 11, then you have increased the value of your building by $36,960 ($3,360 annual increase from pet rent, multiplied by 11). Never forget, improving your full rental income, increases the value to the property.

ADDENDUM TO LEASE

PET AGREEMENT

If you wish to have a pet in your rental unit, you will need to provide the following information and agree to the terms outlined herein. This agreement is an addendum to your lease and a breach of this agreement is also a breach of your rental lease.

Address:_____

_____ Date:_____

_____ I **DO NOT** have a pet. But if I get one, I will let the Landlord or Property Manager know immediately.

_____ **YES**, I do have a pet.

Check the following:

Dog:_____ Name:_____   Weight:_____ Age:____

        Breed:_____

Dog:_____ Name:_____   Weight:_____ Age:____

        Breed:_____

Dog:_____ Name:_____   Weight:_____ Age:____

        Breed:_____

Puppy:_____ Name:_____ Breed:_____

Cat:_____ Name:_____ How Many?_____

Other Types of Animals:

_____Bird(s)

_____Rats, Mice, Hamsters, Guinea pig, Gerbils, Ferret. (Circle all that apply)

_____Snake

_____Fish _____Size of tank (over 10 gallons)

DOGS THAT ARE NOT ALLOWED

- Pit Bulls • Rottweilers • Akitas
- Alaskan Malamutes   • Chow Chows
- Doberman Pinschers • Siberian Huskies
- Perro de Presa Canarios • Boxers
- Wolf-hybrid
- Great Danes
- American Staffordshire Terriers
- Any dog that is a mix of any of the above breeds.

OTHER PETS NOT ALLOWED

- *Farm animals*: Chickens, roosters, goats, pigs, cows, horses, ponies and so on.

- *Uncommon pets*: Monkeys, and/or other endangered or undomesticated animals are not allowed.

PET RENT

- **Dogs (Small):** $35 each per month. Three dog maximum.
- **Dogs (Large, over fifty pounds)**: $50 each per month.
- **Cats**: $35 per month for one cat and $15 for each additional cat. Three cat maximum.
- **Birds**: Caged birds $15 per cage per month. Two cage maximum. Loose birds (Parrot) $20.
- **Rats, Mice, Hamsters, Guinea Pig and Gerbils**: $5 per cage per month.
- **Snake, Lizards, Turtles**: $5 per cage per month.
- **Fish**: $10 per month for a 10 to 55 gallon tank.
- **Ferret**: $25 per month per animal.

Deposits
- Dog: $250 per animal
- Cat: $100 per animal
- All other animals: $50

PETS THAT ARE FREE OF CHARGE
- Seeing eye dog.
- Trained care-giving dog or other pet (training credentials required).
- Goldfish bowl.

Animals that are not on the lease and are staying with Tenant represent a breach of Tenants contractual lease agreement and are grounds for eviction and costs associated to the pet type. Tenant also agrees to care for the animal with regular grooming and baths. If flea, tick or other infestations occur, Tenant is responsible for costs incurred for fumigation and extermination services. Tenant understands that Landlord/Property Manager will not tolerate cruelty or mistreatment of animals and will notify the proper authorities immediately (all costs related to the care and removal of a pet will be incurred by Tenant). Tenant further understands, any animal that management request to be removed from the premises, by written notice from Landlord/Property Manager, must be done so within 3 days.

Tenant has paid the sum of $_____ as a Pet Security Deposit for animals indicated in this agreement.

Tenant has agreed to pay a monthly sum of $_____ as pet rent; this will be added to the monthly rent due as stated on the lease.

All Security Deposits are turned-over in the same timeframe and manner as described in the Lease Agreement. And Pet Security Deposits follow the same conditions as other Security Deposits stated in the Lease Agreement.

It is understood and agreed that Tenant is solely responsible for pets and the Landlord/Property Manager and its agents are not liable for damages to property or bodily harm to individuals.

Tenant: _____ Date: _____
      Signature

Print Name: _____

Tenant: _____ Date: _____
      Signature

Print Name: _____

_____
Landlord/Property Manager   Date

91

Summing Up

Over 50 percent of the population has pets. Landlords that prohibit pets are not only losing extra income that pet owners will pay, but are also excluding a large percentage of the renter population from considering their rentals.

Landlords have to measure the good with the bad regarding tenants with pets. Most pets do not cause problems. Tenants cause the problems with the wrong pets, or basically not taking care of their pets, as they should. And the extra income landlords receive from pet owners is well worth the minimal potential problems.

All pets should be noted on the lease with an attached Pet Agreement.

Chapter 7

Making More with Airbnb

"If you are serious about making as much money as possible landlording, then you've all options. This includes short-term rentals, which have a proved to double and even triple cash flow."

In 2008 Airbnb can on the stage and opened a new way for individuals and landlords to maximize income. Although, they were not the first company to special in the short-stay marketplace, they have become the best known, most popular company of its kind. As I noted earlier, I have starting writing a book, *The Airbnb Hustle*, after realizing that many landlords could benefit greatly with short-term tenants. Not surprisingly, short-term rentals have proven to increase cash flow compared to longer term rentals by two to three times. For instance, if you have a one bedroom, one bath condo in Las Vegas, near the strip that rents for$750 a month, it is likely that you could receive $1,500 to over $2,200 per month as a short-term rental. Does this get you excited? It should, because if you have rentals, whether in popular tourist areas or not, there are always independent business travelers who need options that allow them flexibility with price and accommodations.

There are, however, other website services that cater to short-term stays and vacationers noted earlier in the book that I won't go into here. In this section, we'll stick to Airbnb because it is the one that has the greatest traction as this time. It is the leader in the field with solid customer service and reliability. Their website is easy to navigate and simple to use.

General Background on Airbnb

Airbnb networks in over 34,000 cities and 190 countries. They have over 2 million listing globally and over 60 million guests.

The Airbnb website is user friendly. Most guests and hosts are able to post profiles and reviews of one another.

The Addiction

Using Airbnb is addictive. What I mean by this is that it has opened up a huge Pandora's box to easy access for tourists and business travelers with a vast array of options. As a customer, using Airbnb is easy. One does not have to go to your average hotels or motels. It allows short-term travelers a great opportunity with lodging options and price. When I travel now, I first look to Airbnb to see what is available.

The customer or *guest* base is comprised of vacation renters and business people who are always in need of comfortable and economical lodgings.

If your property is not in a blighted area, you might want to consider the option of turning your rental into short-term or vacation property. You might even consider renting rooms separately. There is a lot to consider here. With engaged service you could yield two to three times as much cash flow than renting your property the traditional way.

With the advent of Airbnd and other short-term services popping up in recent years, proactive landlords have a new and different model for capitalizing and monetizing their investments.

Is it Safe?

Yes, I believe it is safe. Airbnb also has a $1 million protection against damages from guest. This will be explained more as you read on.

Cost of Listing

Listing is free and you only pay 3% on a confirmed reservation. This is a bargain.

Pricing

You are in complete control of what you want to charge. You can also higher and lower your rates during peak times and slower times. For instance, if you have a rental in Las Vegas, you could increase your day rate for a one bedroom condo between December 26-January 1 form $75 to $295. Las Vegas is extremely popular during New Years. You could also increase rates when large conventions are in town, such as the Electronics Expo.

Communicating with Customers

You communicate directly with your customers, with texting, email or phone. You can also checkout your renters and if they are the type of customer you want in your place. You can check there Airbnb feedback from other landlords.

Protection

Airbnb has what they call their The $1 Million Host Guarantee. This guarantee is against damages to your place, should your guest become crazed.

Visit their website for detailed information on this protection.

How Do You Get Paid?

Getting paid is straight forward: When the reservation is confirmed, the guest is billed and you will receive payment 24 hours after your guest has checked in.

What to Rent?

You have many options here and much depends on your location. You could rent the whole place, apartment, house, villa, a Bed and Breakfast Room type: the whole dwelling, private room, shared room.

Other Ideas of What to Rent

- Couch
- Guest House
- Cabin in the woods
- Boat
- Motor Home/Camper/RV
- Mobil Home
- Castel
- Dorm
- Tent
- Treehouse
- Airplane
- Teepee
- Van
- Lighthouse
- Office with couch, cots, Murphy bed

Accommodations

How many people or guest in one rental. When you set up your rental, you will have to decide on how many people you what to accommodate.

Pets

Will you take pets? You could and you could charge more. You can also ask for a larger deposit. You could also restrict different animals and sizes. Most people are conditioned to not travel with their pets; however, you can make a lot more money if you accept pets. You will have to go through all the pros and cons. There is only one advantage--to make more money. But what is the animal has fleas or ticks and now they are in your place. That is not a sight you want to deal with, not to mention other things that could cause major clean up.

Setting Up your Rental

If you have been renting out houses or apartments unfurnished then you will need to furnish them for short-term rentals. You do not need brand new furniture, but you do need contemporary furnishings that are new like and it very good condition. A studio apartment will not cost much to furnish compared to a three bedroom house. The costs could be $1,000 to $5,000. Your costs are speculative because it all depends on the look and quality of the items you want. Remember to make your place very neutral and guest friendly.

Doing into detail here of what you need it beyond this book; however, make are place comfortable. What will you need in the living room, bedrooms, bathroom, kitchen, and in the balconies or patios. You also want to think about cleaning supplies and items that would be used for washing clothes and so on. Envision a first class hotel room. What does it have in it? What does the bathroom have. I have a list of items which I will be including in *The Airbnb Hustle*, for successful Airbnb rentals.

Satellite T.V. and high speed internet access it a must these days.

What Should You Remove?

First off, if you plan to rent your personal residence, you want to remove all personal items from your place (clothes, bathroom items, documents, photos, jewelry, computers, any expensive artwork and equipment that you do not want guess to see or use).

Making Extra Income

Selling DVDs, CDs, books, and video games are a good fit. You can buy great books and other media products from your local library book sale for under $2, most books for $1. Usually these items are donated to the library so you will not have library stamps and stickers on them. You could charge $3 to $4 per item.

97

Selling your Space with Pictures and Pleasant Descriptions

A great picture says a thousand words. Use lots of high quality photos of your rental, inside and out and with all the amenities. If you are renting a condo with a tropical pools and exercise rooms--show them. Also, post photo's of the area, sights and attractions. Show comfort, convenience and beauty.

What to Charge?

Check will other Airbnb rentals in your area and with local hotels. Be competitive with your pricing. You should always be thinking of ways to deliver more for less.

What Amenities to Offer

To get good ideas on how you can make your service better, search the Airbnb site and read other listings. There are unique services some people offer. You might want to offer an airport pickup or drop off service for a reasonable fee. You might want to act as a concierge and take care of show tickets, and other activities. It is all up to you, your time and imagination. If you love to serve and love the hospitality industry, this could be ideal for you. You could offer fresh flowers, fruit basket or lots of bottled water in the room. The amenities you could offer are endless. A good place to start is first ask yourself, "What would I like as an amenity?" Put a list together with prices--and there you have it.

Charging a Cleaning Fee

You should charge a cleaning fee. Most guest will expect it, since nearly all Airbnb hosts charge one. Be realist on your fee and do not overcharge. Search Airbnb site. What are other hosts charging. Also, remember in larger cities, like New York, San Francisco and others, fees are more and guests expect them to be more. To save money, you could do the cleaning yourself.

Duration Minimums and Maximums

Two night minimum and you could determine your own maximum if you want one. In my opinion, as long as there is no problem with the guest, I would not put a maximum length unless it runs into other reservations.

Creating a Professional Listing

Present all the benefits to your rental. And use the descriptive words noted earlier in this book. List everything nice about the property. Go to the Airbnb site and give special attention to the photos and descriptions of hosts with the most booking and best reviews. Search online or get a couple of magazines featuring the best bed & breakfasts. What do the rooms look like? Most people like cozy and warm in the winter and cool and open in the summer.

How Much Can You Make?

You want to shoot for 80% occupancy rate. Once you are at this level, you will make well over three times what you would have made as a long-term rental. Here is an example: You have a one bedroom condo in Orlando, Florida that rents for $650 a month with a one year lease. It is new Disney World so you Airbnb price is $95 per night. If you have your place booked for the entire month (30 days), you gross income is $2,850. Airbnb will take their fee of 3% $($85.5), cable T.V. and internet ($120), condo association ($200), utilities ($100) and $100 for miscellaneous. Let's now say your unit was rented for 80% of the time. Your income is now $2,280. After expense your cash flow is $1,674. This is $1024.50 more than your long-term rent. It's 2.57 times more rent you have received.

Renting Without Owning and Making Money

You can make money from practically anywhere in the world without owning any property. The word here is *control* not ownership. For instance, let's say you have an apartment in San Francisco and it is now July—the middle of summer. Tourists are flocking into San Francisco during the summer. You can sublet your apartment, or a room, or a couch. You do not own your apartment, but you currently *control* the space. Make sense?

Getting Reviews and Communicating with Customers

Great reviews get you more bookings at higher prices. You really want raving fans. Stellar service, actuate descriptions and cleanliness will help. Give more than what is expected. Your guests will measure their experience with value. Don't disappoint them.

Summing Up

The few things I've discussed in this chapter on short-term rentals should have sparked at least some interest to investigate it more. Running a short-term rental puts you into the category of hospitality. You will have to be more proactive and there are services that you will have to provide that as a regular longer-term landlord you will not have to do. But, because of the huge potential cash flow, it might just be worth a try.

Chapter 8

Parting Thoughts

"Success is doing ordinary things extraordinarily well."
—Jim Rohn

Getting your rentals filled fast with solid, long-term tenants is among the most important responsibilities of a successful real estate investor/landlord. Cash flow is king in all businesses and being a landlord and investing in real estate is no exception.

Make increasing cash flow the focus of your rental properties. Think of new ways to create cash flow. Take a piece of paper and write down ideas. Sometimes it is the simple ideas that work the best.

Here are a few things to focus on:

- It is always much easier when your property is updated, clean, and in a desirable location.

- It is equally important that your rent rate is comparable to other rental properties in your area.

- And that management (you) is extremely hands-on with proactive tenant service and aggressive marketing.

- The net you cast will catch the fish you want. The wider the cast, the better selection of fish you'll attract into your net.

Ask yourself the following questions:

- What can I do now to fill my vacancies? Make a list and do the simple things that do not cost much money to perform. (Example: handout flyers at a local self laundry.)

- Write down proactive ways in which you can market your vacancy. Ask these questions: What excites me about my property? Is it totally renovated? Is it in an excellent location? Is it in a family neighborhood with well kept yards and well maintained homes? Is the vacancy spacious, roomy with a big yard? Use all the positives you can think of and put these in your flyer with a couple of great photos of the vacancy.

- What makes renting from you better? Are you more attentive to tenants needs and concerns? Will you jump to solve tenant problems? Will you always make repairs within 24 hours? Are you committed to be an excellent landlord that tenants rave about to friends and family?

- Could you name a few special attributes which you have and other landlords or properties do not? Again, what makes you standout?

- Price isn't always the determining factor to whether your property is rented, but if you are way out of the park given the current market in your area, you will have a tough time getting your property rented. Therefore, do a complete study of rental rates in your area. This should not take more than an hour or two on your computer. Then drive the area and visit other advertized vacancies. Set your price to be competitive. And remember, it is not always the price you want, but what the tenant is willing and capable of paying for the long-term. Your want tenants to be around for five, ten or even twenty years, with a modest increase in rent every year or two. Multi-year tenants are well worth their weight in gold.

102

- Ask yourself: How do I attract long, multi-year tenants? Not having to lose a month of rent or having to repaint or rehab rental units every year will save you thousands of dollars. So, how will you attract long-term tenants? To answer this question, what would you expect from a property or landlord to make you stay for years?

- Numerous things could happen to force a tenant to move: sometimes tenants lose their means of employments, divorce, family tragedy, recessions and depressions occur with economic cycles. How will you combat these occurrences without losing your current rental income? One way may be to adjust your rents to keep units filled. In these types of situations you have to think unemotionally, objectively—business mindedness to keep the income, even though it may be lower, coming in. You cannot afford to have your rentals vacant. You must be broadminded on the price you charge and what you expect to get. Reasonableness is a every landlords gift to a tenant.

- Short-term guests could create the cash flow you have been looking for. With Airbnb, you have a change to grow a real hospitality business with stellar income and repeat customers. There are a lot of advantages with short-term guest with properties in good locations. Visit the Airbnb site and investigate for yourself the benefits. It just might be a perfect fit for you.

One last word and that word is proactive. Be involved. It is easy to not be attached to your rental once it is rented. My monthly checks come in on time and all seems well. You may not even visit your property or hear from the tenants in months. This now is a great passive investment with a perfectly happy tenant. It sounds great doesn't it? And it is. But nonetheless, it is always a good idea to call the tenant, visit the property and see how things are going. Sometimes good tenants will not inform you or problems or potential problem that could cost you a lot of money if ignored. So, be proactive in all of your dealings with your rentals and tenants.

Would You Like to Know More?

You can learn a lot more about real estate investing and landlording in my other books.

What else?

I frequently run special promotions where I offer free or discounted books (usually $ 0.99) on **www.MitchFreeland.com**. One way to get instant notifications for these deals is to subscribe to my email list. By joining you receive updates on the latest offer, you'll also get a free copy of my book "*Mini Goals Huge Results.*"

Check out the link below to learn more.

www.MitchFreeland.com

Did You Like **How to Rent...**

Before you go, I'd like to say "thank you" for buying my book. I know you could have picked from dozens of books on poker, but you took a chance with me. So a big thanks for downloading this book or buying the paperback and reading all the way to the end. Now I would like to ask for a *small* favor.

If you liked this book and found it helpful, could you please take a minute and leave a positive review for this book on Amazon or the site you purchased this book from.

Thank you,
M. Mitch Freeland

What's Next?

The Millionaire Real Estate Flippers is an indispensable resource book that shows you "How to" *Force Appreciation* and Flip Fixer-uppers to capture phenomenal profits.

M. Mitch Freeland and John Freeland know how to flip properties. With *The Millionaire Real Estate Flippers* they show you how to do the same with any property, in any market, in any economy—good or bad.

Explained by professional flippers and long-time investors, this book takes you into the field and up the ladder of real estate investing—*flipping style*. It exposes the good, the bad, and the rightfully ugly, from mild fixer-uppers to the massive "el dumpos," and shows you what to look for and how to profit like the pros.

THE

MILLIONAIRE
REAL ESTATE FLIPPERS

Flipping Fixer-Uppers
How Anybody Can Buy, Fix and Flip Real Estate and Earn a Six Figure Income

"Prolific Investor, John Freeland...finds plenty of properties to buy and sell"
—The Palm Beach Post

M. MITCH FREELAND
JOHN FREELAND

Authors of *The Millionaire Real Estate Landlords*

Let Mitch and John explain the nuts-and-bolts, strategies and methods used to secure a real estate profit plan. This book is the real "stuff" and it is destined to be among an investor's closest companion....Guaranteed!

In *The Millionaire Real Estate Flippers*, you'll learn how to:

- Choose the best type of property starting out
- Fix and renovate on the inexpensive side for maximum profit for small and large fixer-uppers
- What materials to use and how to use them
- Finance your properties quickly
- Hire and manage contractors and sub-contractors efficiently, saving you thousands of dollars
- Inspect property like a pro

- Flip properties profitably every time
- Make 50% + profit on every property you buy
- Locate great deals and turn opportunities into cash cows
- Substantially Increase value to property (what's needed and what isn't)
- Price, list and sell your properties for tremendous profits

Short-term or long-term, seasoned pro or just starting out, *The Millionaire Real Estate Flippers* are to the serious real estate investor as ammunition to a soldier or water to a farmer. This book is a required read for everybody seeking financial freedom and belongs in the library of every real estate investor. And it's on target to be a real estate classic! **GET STARTED TODAY!**

THE MILLIONAIRE REAL ESTATE FLIPPERS

www.MitchFreeland.com

Owning Rental Property Doesn't Have to be Difficult or Stressful

"Make no mistake about it, brothers John and Mitch Freeland are the real deal—no gimmicks here. The…siblings combine business skills with quality service to make for a prosperous real estate investing company."—REIP
The Rewards Magazine

"John Freeland is the Prolific Investor" —The Palm Beach Post

THE MILLIONAIRE REAL ESTATE LANDLORDS

HOW ORDINARY PEOPLE ARE BECOMING EXTRAORDINARY REAL ESTATE INVESTORS & LANDLORDS

How to Manage Single-Family Homes, Duplexes, Triplexes, Quads and Larger Multi-Family Properties for MAXIMUM PROFITS!

M. MITCH FREELAND
JOHN FREELAND

AUTHORS OF *THE MILLIONAIRE REAL ESTATE FLIPPERS*

The Millionaire Real Estate Landlords covers all the essentials necessary for you to achieve maximum performance by utilizing a proactive approach to landlording. If you own rental houses, a duplex, a triplex, quads or other larger multi-family properties, this book will prove that **BIG PROFITS** are attainable for you with the right system.

106

No investor should be without this book. It clarifies and cuts-through the steps needed to succeed in the lucrative world of landlording.

You'll learn the strategies, the techniques of *The Millionaire Real Estate Landlords*—and the hard-driving truths that turn dreams into financial reality with spectacular cash flow.

Here is a sampling of what you will learn in
The Millionaire Real Estate Landlords:

- How to be an extraordinarily effective landlord—AND NOT WASTE TIME!
- How to start from scratch—EVERYTHING YOU WILL NEED!
- Learn secrets behind spectacular cash flow and cash flow management
- How to save money and cut expenses that are meaningful
- How to fully assess an investment for its greatest possible return and its risk to reward ratio.
- How to build contacts with other landlords through real estate investors clubs and associations
- How to access necessary Agreements and Forms you will never see in other real estate books, including many in Spanish that could save you thousands of dollars.

This trend setting book is in a new style, a new era of *"How To"* books on real estate and landlording. With revealing insight, the knowledge you'll gain from *The Millionaire Real Estate Landlords* will carry you successfully and stress-free to the next generation.

Trust Mitch and John Freeland to transform you into a successful property owner, a landlord to be respected, admired and envied.

The Millionaire Real Estate Landlords

www.MitchFreeland.com

SPECIAL SALES

Books published by Las Vegas Book Company are available at special quantity discounts worldwide to be used for training or for use in corporate promotional programs. Quantity discounts are available to corporations, educational institutions and charitable organizations. Personalized front or back covers and endpapers can be produced in large numbers. If you are interested in exploring options for bulk purchase, of ten or more copies, send us an email for discounts.

We encourage you to share this book with others:

- Give this book to friends as a gift
- Give a book to your children or students
- Present this book on your website or blog
- Link your site to www.MitchFreeland.com
- Write a book review for your local paper, your favorite magazine or a website you spend time on. Place your review on Amazon or Goodreads
- Introduce us on radio stations or pod casts—author guest
- Display this book at your shop or business on the counter for resale to customers. Email us at MMitchFreeland@gmail for wholesale rates on bulk orders and volume discounts
- Review a copy for your newsletters, schools papers and magazines, websites, and review journals
- Buy a set of books for the Boys and Girls Clubs in your community, Churches, and fundraising organizations.
- Mention it on your e-mail lists
- Share this book with family members, friends, co-workers and customers who may need a financial boost with a new opportunity
- And share this book with anybody you know who owns rental property

Let me know how I can best serve you.
 For information, contact me at:
www.MitchFreeland.com
MMitchFreeland@gmail

Made in the USA
Middletown, DE
04 October 2023

40188823R00066